THE POWER OF SOMATIC THERAPY

Harness Breathwork, Body Awareness, and Movement to Restore your Mind-Body Connection, Release Stored Trauma and Unleash Emotional Freedom

CLARA HARMON

© Copyright 2024 - All rights reserved.

The content contained within this book may not be reproduced, duplicated or transmitted without direct written permission from the author or the publisher.

Under no circumstances will any blame or legal responsibility be held against the publisher, or author, for any damages, reparation, or monetary loss due to the information contained within this book, either directly or indirectly.

Legal Notice:

This book is copyright protected. It is only for personal use. You cannot amend, distribute, sell, use, quote or paraphrase any part, or the content within this book, without the consent of the author or publisher.

Disclaimer Notice:

Please note the information contained within this document is for educational and entertainment purposes only. All effort has been executed to present accurate, up to date, reliable, complete information. No warranties of any kind are declared or implied. Readers acknowledge that the author is not engaged in the rendering of legal, financial, medical or professional advice. The content within this book has been derived from various sources. Please consult a licensed professional before attempting any techniques outlined in this book.

By reading this document, the reader agrees that under no circumstances is the author responsible for any losses, direct or indirect, that are incurred as a result of the use of the information contained within this document, including, but not limited to, errors, omissions, or inaccuracies.

Contents

Introduction	9
1. AN INTRODUCTION TO SOMATIC THERAPY	**15**
All About Somatic Therapy	15
The Different Types of Somatic Therapy	21
The Principles of Somatic Therapy	23
The Benefits of Somatic Therapy	25
What to Expect on This Journey	28
Interactive Element	29
2. UNVEILING THE SHADOWS—ALL ABOUT TRAUMA	**33**
Defining Trauma	33
The Effects of Trauma on the Brain	37
Trauma and Our Autonomic Nervous System	39
How Trauma Affects the Body	41
What Are the Psychological Effects of Trauma?	44
Interactive Element	45
3. BREATHING LIFE—THE POWER OF BREATHWORK	**51**
Understanding Breathwork	51
Breathwork and Emotional Release	53
Breathing Techniques	55
Integrating Breathwork Into Daily Life	67
Interactive Element	68
4. AWAKENING THE SENSES—MIND-BODY AWARENESS	**71**
What Is Somatic Awareness?	71
The Mind-Body Connection	73
The Role of Mindfulness	82
Interactive Element	87

5. FINDING YOUR GROUND—THE ART OF GROUNDING ... 91
- Grounding and the Science Behind It ... 91
- Grounding Techniques ... 96
- Overcoming Challenges in Grounding ... 103
- Interactive Element ... 105

6. THE DANCE OF RECOVERY—UNDERSTANDING PENDULATION ... 111
- Pendulation Explained ... 111
- Navigating Emotional Waves ... 115
- The Therapeutic Process of Pendulation ... 117
- The Role of Pandulation in Emotional Regulation ... 118
- Interactive Element ... 121

7. BUILDING RESILIENCE—THE POWER OF RESOURCING ... 125
- What Is Resourcing? ... 125
- The Four Es of Resource Therapy ... 128
- Why Resourcing Is Essential ... 130
- Self-Resourcing ... 131
- Cultivating Resources ... 134
- Interactive Element ... 135

8. THE ART OF CONTROL—MASTERING TITRATION ... 139
- Understanding Titration ... 139
- Balancing Emotional Responses ... 145
- Applying Titration in Self-Recovery ... 146
- Interactive Element ... 153

9. SETTING BOUNDARIES—DEVELOPING HEALTHY LIMITS ... 157
- The Importance of Boundaries ... 157
- How to Fortify Porous Boundaries ... 159
- Challenges in Setting Boundaries ... 161
- The Importance and Benefits of Setting Boundaries ... 163

Identifying Boundary Issues	165
Creating Healthy Boundaries	168
When Boundaries Are Violated	170
Interactive Element	171

10. **INTEGRATIVE RECOVERY—COMBINING SOMATIC THERAPY WITH OTHER APPROACHES** — 175

The Holistic Approach	175
Complementary Therapies	180
Confessions: Memories, Trauma, and EMDR	189
Interactive Element	193
Conclusion	197
BONUS CHAPTER: ACTIVITY WORKBOOK	201
Self-Care Practices	201
Gratitude Journaling	204
Positive Affirmations	205
Yoga Poses and Stretches	206
Safety Plan	219
Crisis and Suicide Awareness Protocol	223
References	225

Medical disclaimer

The contents of this book are not intended to replace therapy, diagnose, or cure conditions. All information is provided in good faith with the intent to bring mental, emotional, and physical release, healing, and upliftment. People who experience persistent or severe symptoms of trauma should seek help from a mental health professional, especially if trauma symptoms interfere with daily functioning or social relationships.

Trigger warning

The contents of this book contain themes of depression, anxiety, abuse, post-traumatic stress disorder (PTSD), and trauma. This may be emotionally challenging and upsetting to some readers.

Introduction

> *All emotions, even those that are suppressed and unexpressed, have physical effects. Unexpressed emotions tend to stay in the body like small ticking time bombs—they are illnesses in incubation.*
>
> Marilyn Van Derbur

Toughing It Out for Far Too Long

Do you find yourself dreaming about all the what-ifs or shoulds? How different life would be if it didn't go the way it had or if you could simply take that big step you're scared to take. We all dream of change, freedom, and liberation. How much happier we could be if only we could do this, go there, or be like that. This is something most, if not all people desire and aspire toward. We want to be happy, healthy, and free from the pain and burdens we carry, whether it be physical, mental, or emotional. As much as we long for these, it is often difficult to prioritize the time and ourselves when there is always so much for us to carry or do. Physical and emotional barriers prevent us from achieving most of these goals.

For many of us, the lot we receive in life can be hard to bear and may become heavier as we mature and take on more responsibilities. As our load becomes heavier, we may also be experiencing greater frustrations, heartache, and traumatic events that add to the pain we already have. The barriers that hinder our journey to happiness often lie in the underlying and unresolved trauma we experience throughout life. This includes childhood and adulthood trauma, chronic stress and anxiety from personal relationships and work environments, as well as busy lifestyles or heavy workloads.

All of this serves to distract us from being present and enjoying life and can lead to difficulty in maintaining relationships, isolation and dissatisfaction in life, or feeling unfulfilled. These internal and external factors result in unhappiness and weariness and greatly affect our ability to cultivate happiness in our lives. When most of our days are clouded by these negative events and thoughts, enjoying and appreciating life becomes a distant memory.

Life comes with its own set of hurdles and challenges. No one is exempt from these difficulties, even though it may look as if others are breezing their way through life. The key lies in how we deal with these situations. The way we act, respond to things, and choose how negative events affect us can make all the difference in our day and our perception of ourselves and our reality. You hold all the power in your hands to shape your reality and cultivate a happier self!

Life's obstacles and journeys may make you feel as if you have to go it alone or carry the entire load. The weight we carry can feel heavier on the days when it all gets a bit too much. How much longer do you have to tough it out and take life's punches as they come? Especially, when you feel that you're the last person who should have to go through all of this!

Well, you no longer have to bear the burden on your own. In fact, why not drop a few loads on the wayside? Join this fellowship of people who are taking back control of their lives and happiness one step at a time! There are many methods to help you release stored trauma, pain, and stress that allow you to restore joy and balance in your personal and professional life. Explore this book and improve your mental, emotional, and physical well-being through practices that target these areas and bring healing. Choose to lighten your load today and prioritize yourself again!

Learning to Be Lighter

Have you identified what is standing in the way of achieving your desires? Becoming aware of and labeling these barriers is the first important step on this journey. Addressing what has kept us in a self-destructive cycle or has hindered us from advancing in life brings into focus all that has passed us by or that we missed as life wore us down. It's not too late to turn things around. This book is specifically designed with 10 scientifically proven practices and therapies that can bring relief from pain and trauma and guide you to becoming the best current version of yourself.

Learn to center yourself and promote inner healing through addressing pain points, developing a deeper understanding of decisions made and events that occurred, discovering and rediscovering yourself again, and freeing yourself from emotional burdens that you have carried for way too long. It's your time. Incorporate practices such as somatic therapy, breathwork, mind-body awareness, grounding, pendulation therapy, resource therapy, titration, developing healthy limits, a holistic approach, talk therapy, and interactive therapy, and change the way you have been living. It's time to shift from daily survival to cultivating a lifestyle in which you can thrive and excel.

These somatic therapy practices sap the power from negative emotions and events that may have been holding you hostage and liberate you from them. Choose to incorporate these changes and improve your quality of life in these ways:

- Relieve physical, emotional, and mental pain, and manage post-traumatic stress disorder (PTSD) while reducing stress and anxiety.
- Enhance sleep quality, boost concentration, alertness, and memory, and cultivate present-moment awareness.
- Restore balance, build resilience, and nurture vitality.
- Learn trauma management and coping mechanisms.

- Regulate your nervous system and promote deep relaxation.
- Regulate mood and decrease emotional reactivity.
- Decrease high blood pressure, reduce inflammation, and ease chronic illness symptoms.
- Set healthy boundaries, improve relationships, and recover your sense of self.

Do the aforementioned benefits align with what you once dreamt of achieving? If so, come along on this journey with us. Join countless individuals who are finding and creating the lifestyle they desire. Share your burdens and let them go—you no longer need to bear their weight. Restore and free yourself from all that held you back, and allow yourself to find fulfillment. Release yourself from emotional bondage and pain, reconnect with your mind and body, incorporate mindfulness, and find joy in the little things. Learn to appreciate life again. It's time to make your mental, physical, and emotional health a priority. You deserve it!

ONE

An Introduction to Somatic Therapy

> *The mind-body clash has disguised the truth that psychotherapy is physiology. When a person starts therapy, he isn't beginning a pale conversation; he is stepping into a somatic state of relatedness.*
>
> Thomas Lewis

All About Somatic Therapy

Think back to a time when you were simply going about your day and suddenly something or someone triggers a dark memory or negative emotion you have not experienced in quite some time. It can be the tone of their voice, a hard banging sound, an argument between two coworkers, or even the smell of alcohol that evokes negative emotions, reminding you of an unpleasant past you'd rather forget. The body remembers these events and catalogs your responses. When we experience these negative events and repress them, our body learns to store trauma. Somatic therapy is based on the belief that your body keeps score of traumatic events and unresolved emotional issues (Salamon, 2023). This therapy focuses on your body and the physical and psychological manifestations of emotions.

Through somatic therapy, you will be able to release pent-up trauma, emotions, and negative thoughts that have brought you physiological and psychological pain and illness, kept you in destructive cycles, held you back from achieving your desires, and hindered your ability to build lasting connections. The practices used in your healing journey will include various mind-body techniques that range from breathwork and simple movements like dance and yoga to alternative therapies such as hypnosis and acupuncture. This comprehensive therapeutic approach makes use of resources such as (Salamon, 2023; Silva, 2024)

- encouraging vulnerable conversations with detailed descriptions.
- body awareness to recognize tense areas and soothe them through calming thoughts.
- grounding for mind-body balance and mindfulness.
- pendulation that guides you back and forth between a relaxed state and a stress-inducing state.
- resourcing that encourages you to call upon positive feelings, people, and memories.
- titration that takes you through a traumatic memory takes note of the physical sensation you

experience and talks you through these experiences.
- teaching self-calming tools.
- working through past events with your newly acquired tools.
- strengthening your boundaries.
- incorporating movement and physical expression.
- releasing pent-up emotions.

Somatic Therapy and Talk Therapy

In learning to adapt your emotions, thinking, or behavior and pressing onward in life, you may have come across additional therapies such as cognitive behavioral therapy (CBT). This therapy has achieved great success in working through challenging thought patterns and behaviors to help individuals assimilate to their reality, relieve crippling anxiety, and build confidence. Talk therapies such as CBT mainly focus on the mind, bring awareness of self-sabotaging thoughts, and guide individuals to adopt healthier positive thinking.

Somatic therapy supersedes CBT by going deeper than cognitive penetration and talk therapy and acknowledges the effects negativity can have on the body. Our emotions, negative thoughts, and how we express ourselves (or not) often affect how we physically feel. Experiencing high levels of emotional and mental strain can lead to tension, aches, pain, abdominal upset, and fatigue. In somatic therapy, your body is seen as the threshold for healing. Through this practice, awareness of your body is cultivated as you experience and explore physical sensations, thoughts, memories, and emotions, and use specific resources that alleviate the physical manifestations of stored emotions and trauma.

How Effective Is This Therapy?

In the following three studies, forms of somatic therapy were used to treat and bring mental and emotional ease to many people. A study with set parameters using participants that were randomly divided into groups and then compared with one another found that somatic practices significantly reduced the severity of PTSD symptoms and depression in patients. In another study that included participants who were victims of a tsunami, somatic therapy was proven to be effective and reliable in improving trauma-related symptoms of intrusive thoughts and memories, stress, and avoidance. Additionally, a study on cervical myofascial pain, a condition that causes muscular and connective tissue pain in the neck and shoulder area, found that somatic therapy proved effective in relieving participants' pain (Resnick, 2023).

As seen in the aforementioned three studies, implementing somatic therapy is effective in treating physical and psychiatric issues. Somatic therapy practices improve the emotional and physical expressions of stored trauma in the participants, and it can be just as effective for you.

Who Benefits From It?

Stored trauma can cause debilitating pain and tension, disrupted sleep patterns, exhaustion, and chest tightness.

Somatic therapy works to help us drain negative emotions and unhealthy behaviors that contribute to these physical manifestations. This allows us to go about our days without being shackled to past trauma, memories, and the possibility of experiencing triggers.

Having chronic anxiety or being in a constant distressed state, is like living with your foot on the gas (Salamon, 2023). For many of us, we spend most of our days simply living to make it through another 24 hours. Addressing root causes, developing greater awareness, and building a mind-body connection is a holistic permanent healing. Somatic therapy can alleviate trauma, pain, and tension in individuals who experience the following challenges (Porrey, 2024):

- **PTSD:** Whereas some may see PTSD as a disorder that regularly disrupts bodily functions, somatic therapists observe it as a syndrome, which is a set of traits that commonly occur together and are linked to a particular illness. This means that there is a way to manage and find relief from symptoms experienced by targeting root issues. Somatic therapy benefits such individuals by helping them process trauma and move out of a space that has held them captive.
- **Complicated grief:** Grief encompasses more than cultural and social norms—it is a combination of events that affect us negatively. In addition to death, complicated grief includes job losses, the downfall of relationships, setbacks in life, or even

experiencing a natural disaster. Complicated grief can influence how we function in our daily lives. Somatic therapy addresses chronic pain and physical symptoms associated with prolonged grief and hurtful events.

- **Depression:** Experiencing depression has physical manifestations such as brain fog, listlessness, and back pain. Somatic therapy benefits such individuals by adapting thought processes and using mindful movement.
- **Anxiety:** Somatic therapy can reduce the stress that builds anxious thoughts, grounds individuals, and releases stored emotional and physical discomfort related to stressful incidents.
- **Trust and intimacy issues:** Suppressed trauma can lead to an inability to express ourselves to and be vulnerable with others. Letting go of past hurt and building a greater connection and appreciation for our bodies can help with trust and intimacy issues.
- **Negative body image and self-esteem problems:** When we have a negative self-perception this affects our ability to simply be and accept ourselves. Somatic therapy techniques teach a kinder and more compassionate way of speaking and treating ourselves by eliminating negative self-talk. This helps us develop a more positive perception of ourselves, boosts confidence in our beliefs and capabilities, and motivates us to adopt a healthier mindset for greater self-esteem and improved body image.

- **Addiction and substance abuse:** Building bodily awareness, identifying triggers, and learning present-moment awareness through somatic therapy encourages root-level healing that may help overcome addictions.
- **Panic attacks:** Somatic resources such as detecting and understanding signs of stress and anxiety, meditation, and developing our body-mind connection decrease the intensity and prevalence of panic attacks.

The Different Types of Somatic Therapy

Each of us has experienced different forms of trauma and ways of coping with these events. In life, there is no one-size-fits-all. The holistic approach of somatic therapy is individualized and provides six different therapeutic approaches for you to choose from. Explore these different types of somatic therapy approaches and see which ones align with your needs and level of comfortability.

Standard Somatic Experiencing

Somatic experience therapy uses talk therapy that focuses on paying attention to underlying physical sensations, developing a connection with your body, and working through trauma or stress-related symptoms.

Sensorimotor Psychotherapy

The comprehensive sensorimotor therapy highlights how your body manifests repressed emotions and trauma. This awareness is discovered as therapists draw patients to and from a state of high stress and calm to note any dysregulation they experience. Somatic therapists help to develop greater tolerance, build resilience toward trauma experiences, and build a deeper connection with our bodies.

The Hakomi Method

Hakomi is a form of psychotherapy that helps individuals improve mindfulness and self-awareness to understand their emotions and behavior, focus on their consciousness, and learn to exude loving, positive, and supportive energy to improve healing. This method creates a supportive and calming environment that uses the core concepts of gentleness, compassion, mindfulness, and nonviolence.

Bioenergetic Therapy

Bioenergetic therapy involves bodily movement, such as the use of physical energy and sensations through touch while revisiting traumatic events. This therapy perceives that stored negative emotions can be released through controlled and rhythmic movements or sounds that lull you into a calming and safe space to simply exhale.

Biodynamic Psychotherapy

Biodynamic psychotherapy acknowledges that suppressed traumatic experiences and associated emotions rise to the surface in the form of tightly wound muscles. Alleviating pain and tension in the body and improving blood circulation is achieved through allopathic and holistic practices. Biodynamic therapy combines modern medicine and natural practices to release biochemicals such as lactic acid and adrenaline (Porrey, 2024).

Brainspotting

In brainspotting, somatic therapists identify spots in your field of vision and use this to desensitize you to these associations. When a brainspot is identified, you are guided to fixate on that item or area, recall a traumatic period, and experience those moments again. Brainspotting accesses stored trauma in the subcortical brain which is responsible for our emotions, consciousness, learning, pleasure, and memory. As the root of physical and emotional pain is discovered, the therapist is able to help you work through traumatic events.

The Principles of Somatic Therapy

All events and emotions you experience in life are inscribed in the memory of your mind and body. Somatic therapy is a comprehensive approach because of how it focuses on your physical experiences and encourages you to explore your pain through the use of awareness, feeling, movement, and balance. These four principles are used to encourage health and healing gradually.

1. **Awareness** encourages us to be more attentive and conscious of sensations and emotions in our bodies.
2. **Feeling** highlights and brings understanding to the aforementioned feelings that we have repressed or ignored. In feeling, we no longer have to suppress our thoughts and emotions, but address them and find closure.
3. **Movement** teaches that physical expression can be a way for your body to communicate things we cannot always or that we might struggle to verbalize. Movements such as dance, creativity, or music can be your gateway to expressing yourself emotionally and physically. Not only can movement improve your mood and release feel-good hormones such as serotonin, but it also relieves suppressed feelings in the form of tension in the body as you find freedom in and build a connection with your body in movement.
4. **Balance** observes the duality of the mind and the body. It highlights the importance of balancing mental and physical health through developing mind-body harmony and addressing neglected physical pain or needs. Finding balance helps cultivate a calming environment.

The Benefits of Somatic Therapy

Somatic therapy practices are extremely beneficial for those of us who experience the physical strain of stored emotions and tension daily. Examples of how trauma is trapped in our nervous system can be high-strung emotions and emotional instability, overreaction, hyper-vigilance, hyper-independence, crippling anxiety, panic attacks, stiff necks, locked jaws, and clenched jaws, just to name a few.

Incorporating somatic therapy can benefit you by reducing stress-related symptoms that affect your physical, mental, and emotional health. Somatic therapy aids us in coping with negative thoughts and feelings through developing body awareness, transforming and releasing trauma, building the tools to improve ourselves, releasing tension, relieving ourselves from symptoms effectively, building resilience, freeing ourselves from the past, building emotional awareness, and garnering greater insight into ourselves and our bodies (Integrative Life Center, 2022).

Bodily Awareness

Somatic therapy develops an awareness of your mind and body to target deep-seated trauma stored in your nervous system. Bodily awareness techniques include grounding, resourcing, and body scanning, which observes and acknowledges areas where you carry your pain and tension.

Building Tools for Self-Improvement

When we are burdened by negative emotions and memories, we may find ourselves unable to move forward or find positivity in life. Recognizing bodily sensations and discovering we store unresolved trauma guides us to which tools we should use to improve our physical, mental, and emotional well-being, and change our perception of ourselves and our reality.

Releasing Tension and Transforming Trauma

When we experience trauma, this can lead to PTSD, which causes dysregulation within the body. This emotional dysregulation can disrupt our fight-or-flight response, leaving some of us mentally and physically frozen in fear or anxiety when faced with a hostile environment. Somatic therapy makes use of tools such as trauma awareness and mindful exercises that allow you to expel negative thoughts and emotions. In conjunction with mindfulness, developing body awareness, understanding our physiological responses, and where we store suppressed trauma help reset and regulate systems that went awry.

Effectively Relieving Symptoms

Somatic therapy effectively relieves trauma-related symptoms by focusing on bodily awareness, emotional and behavioral regulation, improved thinking patterns, and renewing your mind to adopt a healthier, positive, and balanced mind-body connection.

Resiliency

The tools you develop through somatic practices are lifelong acquisitions that increase your resilience to overcome future emotional, mental, and physical challenges. Using the practice of pendulation enables you to shift your position from one that is anxious to one that is calm and have the ability to take on life stronger and with greater emotional competence.

Freeing

On this journey, we have to learn to let go of negative self-talk that keeps us from seeing our true reality and becoming present. Negative self-talk greatly influences how we feel, think, and what we believe. In learning to be cognizant of our bodies and the sensations we experience, a nonjudgmental space is needed to truly understand our bodies, give them what they need, and free ourselves from damaging spaces.

Emotional Awareness

Bodily awareness highlights the sensations you experience, where they are located, and what they are related to. This builds emotional awareness that helps you understand your body and what triggers it so that you can make the appropriate changes to improve your physical experiences.

Self-Insight

Somatic therapy helps you finally switch off that autopilot feature and allows you to mindfully take control of your body. Understanding your body and bridging the mind-body connection develops greater insight into how you store trauma, how your body expresses this, and how to leave suffering behind.

What to Expect on This Journey

Embarking on this journey may seem a daunting task. You may be warring with the idea of rehashing traumatic events and the opportunity to live a happier, healthier, and fuller life. Taking part in any form of talk therapy that requires us to be vulnerable is an enormous step to take. Be proud of the courage you've taken in moving in this direction and choosing to take control of your mind and body. Being brave enough to take the first step in confronting traumatic memories can lead to anxious or stressful emotions, but knowing what to expect on this journey ahead of you can help you strengthen your mind and spirit!

Self-reflect and comprehensively assess what your challenges are and what you'd like to overcome. Becoming aware of these areas will allow you to understand which somatic therapies and resources are best for your specific needs and healing journey. This process requires you to be honest, vulnerable, and be able to access detailed memories of traumatic events.

Begin to observe the many ways a negative past affects the way you move, think, behave, breathe, and live. You don't have to be a slave to crippling fear or anxiety any longer. Somatic therapy provides you with tools to navigate and overcome obstacles that try to silence you or crush you underfoot. These therapies will guide you through practices that address suppressed trauma and subsequent emotions and allow you to regain control of your mind, emotions, and body.

Throughout this process, you will create a safe place to express yourself without judgment, shame, or criticism, release negative emotions, build mental and emotional resilience, and nurture a healthy relationship with yourself. Only in this manner, can true effective healing take place (Chamberlain, 2023). On this journey, expect to relive traumatic experiences *and* change how they affect you. Expect to come out the victor.

Interactive Element

Reflective Journal

Journaling is an effective practice for learning and understanding more about your thoughts, emotions, and body. Journals are a way to express your innermost thoughts and desires, be vulnerable without judgment or fear, solve problems, bring clarification and insight, and inspire personal growth. You play the greatest role in determining just how well you excel on this journey.

Instead of suppressing thoughts and emotions, dismissing your needs and health, and surviving daily, starting a reflective journal forces you to be mindful of your feelings and experiences. Reflective journals focus on introspection and change the way you express yourself. Jot down your dreams, daily experiences, and a positive experience. Create plans and set goals to improve your mental, physical, and emotional health outside of therapy. Write down how you feel about this journey and what's expected of you. Use this time to explore your depths and develop a greater relationship with yourself.

How to Start Journaling

Having a reflective journal contributes to changing the way you store trauma and negative emotions—relieving the physical and mental manifestations of it. It is a way to keep score of how you think, feel, and express yourself, and hold yourself accountable for negative self-talk rooted in traumatic experiences. Use these points to start your journaling journey and find freedom in self-expression (Perry, 2023):

- Choose a journaling technique that feels natural to you. It can be in a booklet, on your iPad, or through voice notes.
- Practice self-compassion while journaling. This is a judgment-free zone!
- Be honest in your thoughts and expressions.
- Set realistic goals and take baby steps.
- Create a routine. Set aside quiet time for journaling and spending time with your thoughts. These

periods are not always easy so create an inviting and relaxing space to delve into your emotions and unwind.
- Write whatever thoughts, feelings, and memories that come to mind.
- Express yourself in creative ways, such as artwork or poetry, as long as you let those bubbling emotions rise to the surface.
- Use journaling prompts to unlock thoughts, emotions, and memories.

Prompts for Self-Reflection

Self-reflective prompts are used to stimulate ideas and uncover your innermost thoughts and desires. Often, these prompts may reveal subconscious thoughts and behaviors and bring about greater self-awareness. Answer the following five prompts to begin your reflective journal:

1. What is your happiest memory?
2. How do you handle a negative experience?
3. Do you trust yourself to make smart decisions?
4. What do you like most about yourself?
5. Are you proud of yourself?

Most of us are walking around with some sort of emotional, mental, and physical pain, collecting more baggage, and not knowing how to get rid of it. To get us through the day, we resort to unhealthy coping mechanisms that only bring us momentary relief and we do not deal with the root issue. This is where the true benefit of somatic therapy lies. It targets bleeding wounds and addresses core issues. Somatic therapy helps you confront problems you've allowed to fester and cloud your life, forcing you to address and work through them and let them go. It requires us to face our fears head-on. Learn about the different types of traumas, how they affect you, and how to take charge of negative experiences in the next chapter.

TWO

Unveiling the Shadows—All About Trauma

> *There are wounds that never show on the body that are deeper and more hurtful than anything that bleeds.*
>
> Laurell K. Hamilton

Defining Trauma

Trauma is an emotional response after experiencing a distressing or frightening event. These traumatic events refer to events such as an accident, sexual assault, or a natural disaster. We experience trauma when we are either physically or emotionally threatened or harmed. These events may cause feelings of overwhelm or helplessness, and we may struggle to come to terms with what we've experienced.

Often, these are experiences we have no control over and are difficult to cope with. Trauma can occur at any period of your life and affects each of us differently. It's important to note that not everyone who experiences stressful events will develop trauma. It all goes back to how we process and express ourselves during triggering or traumatic events. Sometimes, the effects of trauma are not known immediately but appear years later when we are triggered or experience similar stress-inducing events (Leonard, 2020).

When we experience trauma and respond by "moving on" in life and making the best of our circumstances, it may feel as if we have dealt with it. But what happens when we experience another traumatic event and use this same coping method? When we experience a series of traumatic events, this can lead to complex or compounding trauma. Complex trauma conditions us to push through when we experience more trauma or when distressing memories resurface. If we don't acknowledge and address what we went through, trauma-associated emotions, fears, and negative feelings become suppressed. When we are triggered, all this stored trauma comes pouring out and because it has not been dealt with, we are overwhelmed with sensations that have us reeling.

Traumatic events and encounters, especially when unprocessed can result in a host of different physical and psychological symptoms. This may depend on the type of trauma that occurred, which may result in either short-term or long-term effects. Trauma types include

- **acute trauma** from a stressful or dangerous singular event
- **chronic trauma** from prolonged exposure to stressful events
- **complex trauma** from exposure to a series of traumatic events

How It Develops

There is no one way to be impacted by trauma. Depending on our temperament, nature, and background, a stressful event can affect each of us differently. There are many different ways in which trauma may develop. Trauma may develop from events that are frightening to you, feeling threatened, being (publicly) humiliated, facing rejection, experiencing abandonment, feeling invalidated, living in an unsafe environment, being in an environment that cyclically moves from a state of distress to calm, feeling unsupported, trapped, or powerless, being ashamed, experiencing direct physical harm or neglect, and secondary trauma from families or communities.

The Different Forms of Trauma

Trauma can be experienced directly or indirectly and may occur in childhood, adulthood, or both. Regardless of the form of trauma, this does not diminish the serious effects that it can have on our bodies. Trauma can occur anywhere and anyhow, and when suppressed, it can lead to long-term pain and discomfort and hinder our personal and social growth. Knowing which form of trauma you experienced and the root of it aids in freeing yourself of trauma-related symptoms.

Childhood Trauma

This is when stress-inducing events such as neglect, emotional abuse, and witnessing physical abuse occur during the impressionable formative years. Such experiences may lead to mental and emotional health problems in adulthood.

Collective Trauma

This is a result of witnessing or being a part of a traumatic event that affects a large number of people negatively. As a result, you may experience social symptoms like increased isolation, anxiety, or cold sweats, especially when you struggle to come to terms with the event or are triggered by memorials dedicated to the event.

Generational Trauma

Generational trauma is a type of trauma that is passed down through generations of a family. It is an event or multiple events experienced by a member or members within the family tree that are remembered and shared with each other and affect family environments, traditions, and behaviors. The legacy of generational trauma can lead to hyperawareness, wariness, hypervigilance, and mistrust of others.

Moral Injury

This is a form of trauma that develops when you are instructed to do a task or forced into a situation that betrays your belief system, values, and morals. You may experience high-stress symptoms as you war with your beliefs and doing what's right or doing what is expected of you. As a result, you may feel shame, anger, or grow to hate your occupation, leading to life dissatisfaction and a lack of purpose.

Secondary Trauma

Individuals who work closely with or witness high-stress events as a part of their job, i.e., paramedics or journalists can experience secondary trauma. This form of trauma can lead to insomnia or feelings of detachment when exposed to such events.

The Effects of Trauma on the Brain

After a traumatic event, our bodies and brains experience long-term effects in the form of health-related *toxic stress*. Toxic stress is the emotional and physical responses we have after being exposed to highly stressful events without fully processing them or receiving the support we need. For instance, when we experience a traumatic childhood, it can affect the way we think, behave, or perceive things. Do you sometimes feel as if you are wired differently when compared to friends who have not experienced some form of trauma? Sometimes, we may struggle to respond appropriately to situations that are seen as normal or non-threatening (Smith-Hayduk, 2022).

Unresolved childhood trauma affects adults in the form of depression, anxiety, emotional dysregulation, and mental health challenges. The latter often leads to difficulties in forming and maintaining positive relationships. If trauma is experienced within the first three years of life, it can greatly affect the development of children's brains. Childhood trauma, stressful environments, or family dysfunction can affect short-term memory and how emotion is regulated. Poor early childhood development may lead to cortisol and adrenaline dysregulation. These hormones are responsible for stress regulation and are important for survival.

Trauma can physically alter the way our brain works by changing our brain's salience network, which is used for learning and survival. Research has found that when our brain is exposed to traumatic events, it compensates for salience networking changes by engaging the executive control network (Smith-Hayduk, 2022). The central executive network is responsible for decision-making, problem-solving, and our working memories. A study by researcher Suarez-Jimenez, his fellow co-authors, and senior author Neria found that patients with PTSD are able to complete the same tasks as individuals who were not exposed to trauma, as long as it was completed with indifference (Smith-Hayduk, 2022). When patients with PTSD were emotionally triggered or felt threatened, they were unable to complete these tasks. It was discovered that trauma resulted in fewer signals shared between the hippocampus, which is responsible for our emotions and memory, and the salience network. Additionally, less communication was observed between the area of the amygdala, where the brain is linked to emotion, and the default mode network. The default mode network is activated during periods when we focus less on activities happening around us. This study revealed that individuals with PTSD were unable to distinguish between moments of stress and unstress; they overgeneralized danger and became overwhelmed with emotions, which hindered their cognitive ability.

Trauma and Our Autonomic Nervous System

The autonomic nervous system (ANS) consists of two separate but interconnected systems: the sympathetic and parasympathetic nervous systems. These systems aid in regulating the body's response to threats.

Sympathetic Nervous System

The sympathetic nervous system (SNS) is your fight-or-flight system that prepares the body to respond to stressors or danger by activating various physiological responses. These SNS responses may be (Cohen, 2023)

- increasing your heart and respiratory rate
- dilating airways for increased oxygen intake
- releasing cortisol (stress hormone)
- redirecting blood flow away from nonessential functions, i.e., digestion to muscles and vital organs
- sharpening your alertness and attention

Parasympathetic Nervous System (PNS)

The parasympathetic nervous system (PNS) is your rest and digest system that counteracts the responses of the SNS by inducing relaxation, calm, and recovery. To conserve energy and bring calm to your body, the PNS responds by (Cohen, 2023)

- decreasing your heart and respiratory rate
- constricting your airways
- improving digestion and nutrient absorption
- promoting a restful state

ANS and Fight-Or-Flight Responses

The way our body responds to threats or danger is an innate survival mechanism. Your fight-or-flight response can be traced back to your ancient ancestors who thrived in a dangerous environment and had to hunt for their survival. The adrenaline produced sharpened their senses, increased their alertness, and guided them to either take a defensive stance or flee and find shelter. Once the danger had passed, their body systems would return to normal.

When we face threats in our current life, such as a distressing work environment, overwhelming responsibility, or a fast-paced life, this age-old instinct is ignited. When compounding trauma and distress dysregulate our SNS, this keeps us on a perpetual high alert with a continual flow of cortisol in our bloodstream. You may experience this in the form of crippling anxiety, panic attacks, or ruminations about the many things that could go awry around you. Remaining stuck in this heightened state makes it difficult to stimulate the PNS and ease your body.

How Trauma Affects the Body

Physical and emotional pain may make it hard to cope with life. When we are in a constant state of stress, our bodies experience exhaustion a lot more often. To deal with unresolved emotions related to a traumatic event, we may find ourselves relying on unhealthy practices. Although this can bring temporary relief, allow us to find momentary pleasure, and simply forget for a while, it prolongs the impact that trauma has on our minds and bodies. Traumatic experiences and unprocessed trauma affect many different areas of the body.

Experiencing trauma affects our body's central stress response through sensitizing the hypothalamic-pituitary-adrenal (HPA) axis. The HPA axis connects our central nervous system and our endocrine system, making us more reactive to stress and increasing the production of the stress hormone cortisol. Cortisol is responsible for increasing sugar in our bloodstream, enhancing how the brain uses glucose, and increasing the availability of tissue-repairing substances (Basile, 2020). An overly-sensitized HPA axis can lead to the dysregulation of cortisol which keeps us in a revved-up state. Chronically high levels of this stress hormone increase the risk of heart disease, inflammation, anxiety, and depression.

In addition to dysregulating adrenaline and cortisol, trauma affects the hormone oxytocin. Oxytocin affects mood, social and relationship bonding, trust, and affection, and increases attraction. Experiencing trauma during the early stage of life can affect the regulation of oxytocin (Basile, 2020). Possible results of childhood trauma on oxytocin are detachment, difficulty with affection, and heightened anxiety in later years. Low levels of oxytocin may lead to decreased resilience and poor adaptability in life.

After a traumatic event, the first adverse effects of unprocessed trauma we observe are depression, anxiety, anger, or the belief that the world is unsafe, and it may even alter our personalities as a coping mechanism. These psychological effects disrupt our daily lives and could distort our perceptions of the traumatic event experienced and our current reality. The psychological effects of trauma are not immediate and may appear after several months or years. The leading indicators of psychological trauma include (Khoddam, 2021)

- re-experiencing traumatic events
- distressing memories and nightmares
- emotional detachment
- avoiding physical reminders of trauma, i.e., places, people, or activities
- a persistent state of arousal, i.e., being tightly wound for much of the day, sleep disruptions, poor concentration, and becoming easily irritated
- negative changes to our thinking and mood

There are different ways that the brain responds to trauma. Major traumatic experiences that occur when we are emotionally, mentally, or physically vulnerable can root us in a fear response state that traps us in our body. We can become fearful of our environment and constantly expect bad events to happen whenever we leave the comfort of our safe place. Such experiences may lead to panic attacks, obsessive-compulsive disorder (OCD), and chronic pain. PTSD-related symptoms can show up in the form of

- persistent feelings of overwhelm
- muscle tension
- chest tightness
- edginess
- brain fog
- disassociation

As a result of trauma or a series of traumatic events, dysregulated body responses and an impaired fight-or-flight response can leave some of us in a frozen state. A freeze response is an unconscious cognitive and behavioral act that occurs when we experience threats. In these moments, you may not know what to do or how to act which can leave you feeling powerless or hopeless. A freeze response may result in blank spots in your memory as your mind blocks out what happens during trauma. Memories may seem confusing or disordered, and some may not have memories of the event for years.

After a traumatic experience, the body relieves high-strung emotions and tightly wounded muscles as it tries to reset and regulate itself. Chemicals are released to calm the body after a threat is removed. Experiencing high tension and moving to a relaxing state can feel as if you are crashing down. You may feel exhausted and your muscles may be tender.

What Are the Psychological Effects of Trauma?

Stressful events activate your fight-or-flight response and cause your body to take a defensive stance. Your body's stress response can lead to physical reactions such as raised blood pressure, increased heart rate, increased sweating, a loss of appetite, or nausea. Intense emotions and your body's swift response can lead to experiences of shock, denial, anger, or sadness as your body winds down.

Some individuals will recover and move past such events gradually, but for those who experience the aforementioned symptoms persistently and are plagued by flashbacks of the event, mental health concerns may develop. In many cases, common emotionally traumatic experiences such as verbal abuse, death, bullying, separation, and neglect lead to psychological problems. As a result, you may find yourself experiencing the following psychological effects (Pagán, 2018):

- crippling anxiety that plagues your every waking moment and keeps you in a stressed state
- reliving traumatic moments and emotions, which result in nightmares and disrupted sleep
- behavioral changes such as a change of routine or the use of coping substances that lead to maladaptive and destructive behavior
- health issues as a result of constant high stress levels that cause inflammation in your body and may lead to cardiovascular or autoimmune diseases

- poor cognitive function such as problems with memory and concentration as your brain struggles to deal with emotional trauma

Interactive Element

Trauma Timeline

The first step in addressing trauma so that you can begin to release it and bring balance to your mind and body is to find the source of your trauma. When did it begin? What caused it? Is it a singular event or a series of them? Is your trauma connected to one individual or a group of people? These questions are important to finding healing and redefining how trauma affects you. One way to depict significant life events and uncover potential traumas can be to use a timeline chart. Timeline charts are used to chronologically visualize a set of events. When you use a timeline, you are able to see events in sequence and understand their impacts. Trauma timelines are a moment for you to reflect on what you've survived.

How to Construct a Timeline

When preparing to design or fill in a trauma timeline, it's important that you are in the proper headspace where you can allow yourself to revisit the past. This process requires you to fully delve into events you'd rather not remember and try to capture pivotal moments that caused high levels of stress, anxiety, or anguish. Be specific, detailed, and honest with yourself as you allow memories to resurface.

Trauma timelines consist of a sequence of prompts and blank spaces to guide you in releasing and vocalizing trauma you have long since repressed. Here's how you can start:

1. Create or use a designed timeline chart.
2. For each row, jot down a specific traumatic event in your life.
3. Write down a title for each event and describe it.
4. In the following block or row, describe the emotions resulting from the event.
5. Fill in the physical reactions you experience.
6. Describe any triggers you have developed as a result of this trauma.
7. Write down the ways you use to cope.
8. Replicate this chart for each traumatic event experienced to help process multiple events.

Use the QR codes below to generate templates that you can use to construct and complete your trauma timeline.

Childhood Trauma Timeline

Adulthood Trauma Timeline

Why Trauma Timelines Are Beneficial

It's not easy to face events that are traumatizing but the longer we hold it all inside, the greater our physical, mental, and emotional pain becomes. As your trauma timeline details a painful history, you are able to identify distorted self-beliefs and change them. Timelines enable you to assess what coping mechanisms you have used and whether or not they have benefitted you or added to your pain. Recognizing how trauma has affected us, the lasting impact it has on our health and bodies, and how it possibly still affects our daily lives is important to our healing process. For many individuals, highlighting how trauma has controlled their lives for so long, motivates them to take their power back.

Prompts to Guide Your Trauma Timeline

When you think back on a traumatic event, it is easy to see it as one giant event and become overwhelmed by the emotions we associate with it. Using prompts can help us dissect our memories and understand associated emotions and physical reactions. Use the five prompts below to help you reflect and bring understanding to the effects of trauma.

1. How has what you experienced negatively affected your personal relationship?
2. Do you resent the person or people responsible for the trauma you've experienced?
3. How has trauma changed the way you approach life?
4. What do you do when negative memories resurface?
5. What positive habits can you adopt to counteract the negative effects of trauma?

Trauma can have a decades-long hold on individuals. It affects the way we talk about ourselves and to others, how we move through life, which opportunities we embark on (or not), the amount of love and positivity we accept from others, our beliefs and self-esteem, and how fulfilling we find life. Trauma can have us feeling stuck and unsatisfied, eventually keeping us in a negative, self-destructive, and pained state. When we suppress traumatic events, our bodies take the brunt of it. It results in psychological, emotional, and physical challenges that lead to further unhappiness, isolation, hormonal imbalances, depression, crippling anxiety, and heightened fearfulness. When we are plagued by these trauma-related symptoms, we are unable to live the life we desire or deserve.

In understanding and addressing trauma, you are one step closer to escaping the bonds that such events may hold you hostage in. When we face these experiences, we are choosing to no longer be tethered to a past that negatively dictates our present and future. Once you become aware of how it has affected your body, you can begin the process of eliminating adverse symptoms and physical reactions that are hindering your personal growth. Breathwork is one of those somatic practices that brings you back into alignment with your body and helps you regulate what trauma has dysregulated.

THREE

Breathing Life—The Power of Breathwork

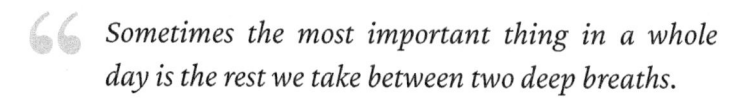

> *Sometimes the most important thing in a whole day is the rest we take between two deep breaths.*
>
> Etty Hillesum

Understanding Breathwork

Think back to a time when someone tried your temper. Perhaps, you took a moment to inhale and hold your breath—calming your raging thoughts and racing pulse. Instead of responding in anger, you held your breath and slowly exhaled in order to respond in a kinder manner. Did you know that you just unintentionally participated in breathwork practices? Somatic breathwork highlights how breathing can influence emotions and how emotions can affect how we breathe. This mind-body practice emphasizes how our physical sensations are connected to our mental and emotional states. Breathwork is built on the principle that becoming aware of how we breathe and modulating it can lead to self-improvement, reduce stress, and make emotional healing possible (Cohen, 2023).

The therapeutic practice of breathwork includes various breathing techniques, such as deep and rhythmic breathing to techniques with specific patterns that promote physical, emotional, and mental health (Cohen, 2023). Breathing can be done intentionally and when we change our rhythms, our internal feelings and our emotional state can be altered. Breathing intentionally signals the parasympathetic nervous system to move from a state of stress to one that is relaxed. This allows us to experience negative or big emotions without being trapped in grief, sorrow, hurt, shame, or despair.

The Benefits of Somatic Breathwork

Somatic breathwork achieves mental and emotional well-being by stimulating the parasympathetic nervous system (PNS). Breathwork has the ability to heal us by reducing stress and improving our overall health. It improves cardiovascular health, mental clarity, digestion, and sleep quality, while reducing blood pressure, cortisol, blood glucose, and tension in the body by directly affecting the PNS (Kiersten, 2023).

Deep or slow breathing leads to improved mood and less anxiety and provides nourishment to tissue cells. When done regularly, studies have shown that consistent breathwork increases oxygen consumption by 37% (Hadley, 2023). In a study that examined the effects of breathwork on stress and mental health, 40 participants were randomly assigned to either a breathing intervention group or a group that received no intervention, i.e., the control group. This study found that breathing intervention resulted in less cortisol production, improved sustained attention, and a significant decrease in negative affect (Tucker, 2023). This was not observed in the control group.

Breathwork and Emotional Release

Breathwork incorporates the belief that trauma can be released by reversing the order of the stages in SNS responses using techniques such as breakthrough breathwork, rebirthing breathwork, and holotropic breathwork. Holotropic breathing brings you to an altered state through even breathing patterns and repetitive movements to break through trauma-related mental and emotional blocks. Slowly inhaling and gradually escalating to a more rapid breathing rate activates the SNS and takes us to a distressed state.

During this state, you may experience flashbacks to a traumatic event, which allows you to confront emotions, thoughts, and events. This experience may lead your body to display the physical effects of unlocked trauma such as muscle tension or the need to flee, but as you learn to hold your breath, you will be able to release these emotions and bring relief to your body. Exhaling often brings along feelings of joy or lightness (Hills, 2023). Breathwork helps us to address and manage difficult emotions, redirect the flow of emotions, and release stored trauma.

Breathwork and Panic Attacks

Panic attacks are triggered by trauma-related events, objects, sounds, or people that cause us extreme anxiety and distress. When we experience panic attacks, our bodies are taken to a heightened state where normal responses to danger, stress, or excitement are exaggerated. In such events, you may feel as if you are losing control of your mind and body, having a heart attack, or knocking at death's door. During a panic attack, our breathing becomes shallow and irregular, making it difficult to take in the air we need. You may experience sensations such as (Princing, 2021)

- lightheadedness or dizziness
- a very hot or very cold body temperature
- a racing heart, increased sweating, or trembling
- nausea
- a pounding heartbeat
- tightness or pain in your chest or abdominal discomfort
- difficult catching your breath
- jelly-like legs
- a disconnect from your environment

Deep breathing allows us to take in more air which induces calm and reduces anxiety. This form of breathwork involves taking long deep breaths, the opposite form of breathing that occurs during panic attacks.

Breathing Techniques

There are a host of different breathing techniques that can benefit you and that work with your level of comfort. Let's explore the different popular breathing techniques below!

Resonant Breathing Exercise

Resonant breathing reduces symptoms of depression and boosts your mood. This breathwork practice requires you to (Kirstein, 2023)

1. Sit upright on a flat surface, place one hand on your chest, and the other on your abdomen.
2. Inhale for five seconds through your nose and feel your belly expand.
3. Hold your breath for one to two seconds.
4. Exhale for five seconds through your nose and feel your abdomen deflate.

As you repeat this routine for two to five minutes, keep your breath smooth and steady. Become aware of how your abdomen expands and deflates as you breathe. As you fall into the rhythm of this breathwork, use this opportunity to release troublesome thoughts and distractions.

Diaphragmatic Breathing Exercise

Diaphragmatic breathing

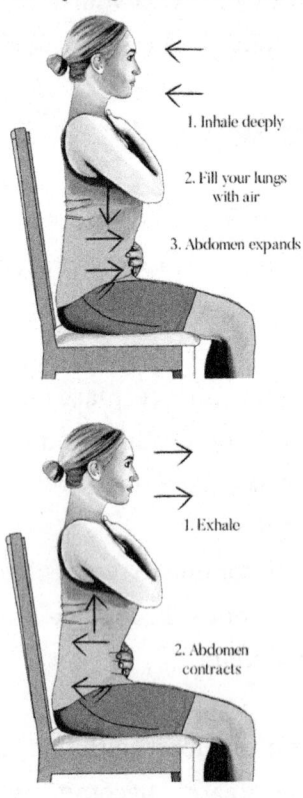

1. Inhale deeply
2. Fill your lungs with air
3. Abdomen expands

1. Exhale
2. Abdomen contracts

Diaphragmatic breathing strengthens our diaphragm, improves sleep, and activates the PNS to facilitate healing breathwork for emotional health. In this exercise (Kirstein, 2023)

1. Place one hand on your chest and the other on your upper belly.
2. Slowly inhale through your nose.

3. As you inhale, become aware of how your belly is expanding. Feel your ribs expand and push your diaphragm downward.
4. Exhale slowly through pursed lips and relax your belly.
5. Still your chest and engage in deep core breaths, expanding your belly.
6. Repeat this exercise for two to five minutes.

Box Breathing Exercise

Box Breathing

inhale
1, 2, 3, 4

hold
1, 2, 3, 4

exhale
1, 2, 3, 4

hold
1, 2, 3, 4

Box breathing stimulates the PNS, promotes relaxation, and lowers blood pressure and heart rate. Follow these steps to practice this exercise (Kirstein, 2023).

1. Visualize drawing a square while sitting upright.
2. Inhale through your nose for four counts and outline the square's first side.
3. For the next four counts, hold your breath until you have completed tracing the second side.
4. Release your breath for four counts and make your way across the third side.
5. Hold your breath once more for four counts as you outline the fourth side.
6. Repeat this exercise for three to five minutes, using equal breaths that are smooth and rhythmic.

Sound Stimulation Breath Exercise

Sound Stimulation Breath

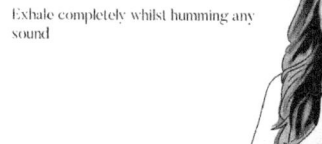

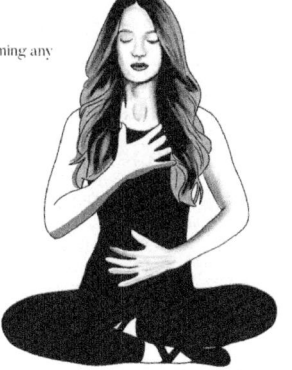

Inhale deeply

Exhale completely whilst humming any sound

Sound stimulation breathing uses resonance healing to release tension and create mental clarity. This exercise requires you to (Kirstein, 2023)

1. Sit comfortably and place your hand on your lower abdomen.
2. Hum a single note as you inhale and exhale slowly through your nostrils

3. Build awareness of the vibrations you experience as your abdomen expands.
4. Repeat this exercise for two to five minutes as you focus on the sensations you feel and emit.

Breath Awareness Exercise

Breath awareness cultivates mindfulness through conscious breathing. In this exercise (Kirstein, 2023)

1. Close your eyes or soften your gaze as you find a comfortable position.
2. Become aware of your natural breathing rhythm.
3. Observe each inhale and exhale.
4. Try not to let your mind wander and maintain present-moment awareness.
5. Visualize each inhale as drawing in positive energy and each exhale as releasing frustrations, distractions, or tension.
6. Repeat this exercise for two to five minutes.

Breathing Life—The Power of Breathwork • 61

Somatic Nostril Breathing Exercise

Somatic nostril breathing

Plug right nostril.
Inhale through left.
Plug left nostril.
Exhale through right.

Inhale through right.
Plug right nostril.
Exhale through left.
Repeat.

Somatic nostril breathing teaches us to balance energy, which aids in relieving anxiety and reducing stress. This exercise requires you to (Kirstein, 2023)

1. Sit with your left hand placed on your knee.
2. Close your right nostril with your right thumb, and inhale slowly through the left nostril.

3. Close your left nostril with your ring finger, and exhale through your right nostril after removing your thumb.
4. Repeat this exercise and continue alternating nostrils for two to five minutes.

The Anxiety-Busting Breath

The anxiety buster incorporates humming and focuses on exhalation. This exercise requires you to (Brooks, n.d.)

1. Sit or lie quietly.
2. Inhale deeply.
3. Lengthen your exhale as you breathe out with gentle humming.
4. Ensure that your exhale is longer than your inhale and continue humming.

Rib Pliability Somatic Breathing Exercise

Rib pliability breathing brings awareness to the movements of your abdomen and rib cage. This exercise requires you to (Brooks, n.d.)

1. Be seated or standing.
2. Notice how your rib cage moves and expands on the side as you breathe.
3. Reach your left hand across your abdomen and place it on the lower side of the right rib cage.
4. Place your right hand on the opposite side.

5. Move your arm positions from the placement above to a relaxed state and return your arms to their sides.

Using little effort, move your arms back and forth from these positions, and take note of how your rib cage moves with your arm. Repeat this exercise 5 to 10 times and observe changes in your breathing.

Breath of the Cell Exercise

Breathwork of the cell encourages us to awaken our senses and our cells by paying attention to the subtle movements in our body which helps us feel more alive and connected. In this exercise (Brooks, n.d.)

1. Lay down in a comfortable position and place.
2. Imagine that you are floating and feel the air around you.
3. Become aware of the air changes around you and imagine that the pores on your skin are open.
4. Visualize and feel as they begin to close.
5. Repeat this expanding and contracting and find a rhythm.
6. Take note of how your breathing changes.

Stop Holding Your Breath Exercise

This breathwork practice remedies breathing habits that cause us to hold our breath in anxiety and instead brings us back to the present. This exercise requires us to (Brooks, n.d.)

1. Place one hand on your chest and the other on your belly.
2. Breathe as you normally do.
3. Take note of where you are, what you're feeling, or even the floor beneath your feet to ground yourself.
4. Inhale and exhale effortlessly without taking deep or big breaths.
5. Find a calming rhythm and simply breathe with ease.

Connected Breathing

This exercise is gentle circular breathing that can be done either sitting in a chair or lying on your back, utilizing nostril breathing, i.e. breathing in and out of the nose. As you complete this exercise, you may notice lightheadedness and tingly sensations as your PNS is stimulated. Connected breathing is a gentle exercise using nostril breathing that requires you to

1. Sit comfortably with your feet flat on the ground or lying on your back with a supported neck and knees.
2. Have no restrictions around or in front of your abdomen.
3. Inhale deeply without pausing and relax your exhale.

4. Continue to inhale and exhale while pausing at the top or bottom of your breath.
5. Repeat this exercise for 10 to 20 connected (circular) breaths and notice a change in how you feel.

Reset Breath

Reset breath is designed to help us become present and less stressed through a simple body breathing tool. It improves our focus, attention, and well-being and helps to clear emotional static. This exercise brings balance to our autonomic nervous system function. Reset breathing uses intentional and relaxing breathing that improves attention, helps us to be present, and removes emotional static (Youst, 2016). This exercise requires you to

1. Sit comfortably.
2. Take two to three deep, cleansing breaths through the nose.
3. Exhale calmly through your mouth and release stored tension.
4. Place one hand on your belly and the other on your chest and take in 10 full breaths.
5. Feel how your breath rises from your belly and flows into your chest.

There are three different ways to perform this exercise and you can incorporate whichever one is more comfortable to do:

1. Breathing in and out through your nose
2. Breathing in through your nose and out through your mouth
3. Breathing in and out through the mouth

Relax and Recenter

Relax and recenter allow you to reach maximum relaxation and regulate the connection between your mind and body. It releases emotional tension and stress, promotes mindfulness, and re-centers through aligning respiratory and circulatory functions. Using four-by-four breathing, this exercise requires you to do the following 4 steps.

Step One: Sigh

1. Place one hand on your belly and the other on your chest.
2. Inhale deeply, expanding your belly, and exhaling in one big whoosh of a sigh.
3. Repeat this part four times.

Step Two: Squeeze

1. Breathe in a deep belly-chest breath through your nose.
2. Release your breath through your nose and mouth, and begin tightly squeezing your abdomen halfway through this exhale.
3. In the next moment, release all tension in your

abdomen, pushing your belly outward, and simultaneously begin inhaling once more.
4. Repeat this exercise four times.

Step Three: Stop

1. Following the last breath above, relax your abdomen and begin to inhale.
2. Inhale deeply to the count of four.
3. Hold your breath for four counts.
4. Gently release your breath with a controlled exhale for eight counts.
5. Repeat for four cycles.

Step Four: Center

1. Inhale for eight counts and exhale for the same amount.
2. Center yourself and incorporate mindfulness.
3. After completing this circular breathing, bring yourself back into the present.

Integrating Breathwork Into Daily Life

The lasting and true benefits of breathwork come with regular incorporation. Ensuring we breathe well is important to counteracting stress-inducing breathing patterns that stimulate our SNS and increase anxiety levels. The best way to promote a calming and relaxing state that allows us to enjoy our surroundings and find positivity is to incorporate breathwork into our everyday lives. Here are five ways to do just that!

1. Create a routine in which you practice daily breathwork. It can be the first thing after you wake up, before you exit the car and walk into work, before and after conducting a presentation, or after returning from a busy day outside. Routine allows breathwork to become your second nature.
2. Find or create comfortable and safe environments where you can practice breathwork without stress or anxiety being triggered.
3. Do not incorporate breathwork too often or for too long. Let it feel natural and utilize it appropriately.
4. Set a digital reminder for breathwork practices to maintain a routine, prioritize your breathing, and motivate you to retrain your mind and body.
5. Use breathwork anywhere and anytime. Incorporate while you do your grocery shopping, driving, or as you shower.

Interactive Element

Pick a Breathing Technique

Of the many breathwork techniques mentioned above, choose one that piques your interest. Incorporate this exercise for one week, using the daily incorporations above. Take note of any differences you experience and write them down. If you feel that your first pick did not produce the results you desired, try different breathwork techniques until you come across the one that you get the most out of. After engaging in these exercises, use the prompts below to journal this experience.

Prompts for Breathwork

During breathwork exercises, different emotions and memories may resurface. As you exhale mental, emotional, and physical stressors or tension, you may develop greater self-understanding and mental clarity. Use these prompts to uncover realizations and find release.

- I experience great anxiety when...?
- I am not...?
- Where do you notice that your body stores stress?
- I felt my worst at...?
- How do you allow childhood trauma to affect my adulthood?

Breathwork is a breakthrough practice altering the way our body reacts to uncomfortable situations. By focusing on how our body reacts to threats and cultivating mind-body awareness, we can reverse the overwhelming effects of unprocessed emotions and trauma. Breathwork is a way to reset our mind and our body, regulate our nervous system, and heal our overall health. Breathwork is important to mitigating emotional trauma and changing our emotional reactions which builds greater resilience to life's challenges.

Explore the different techniques of breathwork, find your calming rhythm, and experience a sense of peace you have not felt in quite some time. The body awareness that awakens through breathwork is pivotal to finding balance and restoration after trauma.

FOUR

Awakening the Senses—Mind-Body Awareness

> *Body awareness not only anchors you in the present moment. It is a doorway out of the prison that is the ego.*
>
> Eckhart Tolle

What Is Somatic Awareness?

Somatic awareness is the intentional act of becoming conscious of sensations in your body (Morgan, 2021). As you become aware of your body, you are creating and strengthening your relationship with it and your mind. This lifestyle practice makes us conscious of new and chronic positive or negative sensations and guides us into addressing them. Instead of becoming overwhelmed with or carried away by emotions and heightened physical reactions, embodiment allows us to take note of how our body is reacting to stressors or threats. Mind-body awareness helps us to recognize whether our body's reaction to these events matches the danger of the threat and, if not, find ways to reset our physiological responses. Pausing to listen to our bodies and recognize these physical reactions, guides us to self-regulation.

The Benefits of Somatic Awareness

Incorporating somatic awareness provides more than momentary relief. Incorporating this somatic exercise and becoming mindful of your body, improves your psychological state, physical health, and interpersonal relationships. Here are the six ways that somatic awareness can benefit you:

1. **Relieves stress:** Through mindfulness and body scanning, we take note of how the physical responses of stress manifest in our bodies and learn to counteract these sensations with a calming approach.
2. **Helps regulate emotion:** Recognizing your emotional responses to negative environments and connecting with them allows you to soothe yourself by stimulating the rest and digest function of the parasympathetic nervous system.
3. **Releases tension in the body:** Becoming cognizant of your mind, emotions, and body releases stored trauma that causes chronic aches and tension in the body. This is achieved as we identify where pain in the body manifests and target these areas. As you unlock stored emotions and unburden yourself,

your body becomes less stressed and you can release tense muscles.
4. **Improves self-esteem:** Mindfulness and developing mind-body awareness restores your relationship with yourself. It builds and strengthens your appreciation and acceptance of yourself, teaches self-compassion, and allows your personal relationships to flourish.
5. **Builds resilience:** Mental and emotional perception are strengthened which improves your resilience against life's challenges and others' negativity. A mind-body connection and understanding allow you to cope with difficulty, overcome stressors, and become emotionally competent.
6. **Cultivates present-moment awareness:** Somatic mindfulness meditation brings a wandering or overwhelmed mind back into the body and the present. Present-moment awareness halts us from being carried away by anxiety, overthinking, or self-criticism.

The Mind-Body Connection

The mind-body connection observes that how we feel, what we believe, and the attitude we approach life's obstacles with can negatively or positively affect how our bodies function and respond. What we eat, listen to, participate in, and believe about ourselves matter. It can affect both our minds and our bodies. Our subconscious and conscious mental states affect our bodies. An overly anxious or stressed mental state causes adrenaline and cortisol dysregulation that can weaken our immune responses, cause digestive problems, and decrease the rate at which we heal. The mind-body connection is important to creating physiological and psychological balance so that the body is able to work at optimal levels.

Why We Experience Mind-Body Disconnection

Our mind and body are interconnected and dependent on each other. When one is neglected or they are no longer in sync, there is a disconnect. This is often the result of trauma, unprocessed emotions, stress, anxiety, and depression. Symptoms of mind-body disconnection may be pain, fatigue, or digestive and gut problems. You may feel unfulfilled and numb to your environment and begin to disassociate from your reality. Mind-body disconnection can affect your personal and work life by impacting your motivation and productivity.

These are the signs that you may be disconnected (Egel, 2021):

- You struggle to connect with or understand what you are feeling and why, cannot label it, or are detached from emotional expression.
- You over plan and make sure that you are always busy, leaving no time to experience or address emotions. A full schedule allows you to avoid difficult emotions and thoughts.

- You are too hard on yourself. High and unrealistic self-expectations often have you shaming or criticizing yourself. You need to take your mental, physical, and emotional state into consideration. Learn to be flexible and reduce the stress you place on yourself.
- You are hyper-focused on what you should be or look like, not taking into account your reality and individuality. There is no one-size-fits-all regimen, diet, or exercise. Move at your own pace and learn to listen to your body's signals without pushing it too far and keeping your challenges in mind.

Listening to Your Body

When we have many tasks and responsibilities, lots of outside noise, or are plagued by negative thoughts and emotions, it can be difficult to hear our body's signals and needs. Somatic therapy forces us to prioritize ourselves and take moments to be still and breathe. In these moments, you may notice sensations in your body, such as a clenched jaw, holding a rigid stance, or tense shallow (upper chest) breathing. Listening to your body utilizes awareness techniques such as tapping, progressive muscle relaxation, and body scanning, which enables you to fine-tune your listening skills and understand the messages your body sends.

Tapping

EFT Tapping Points

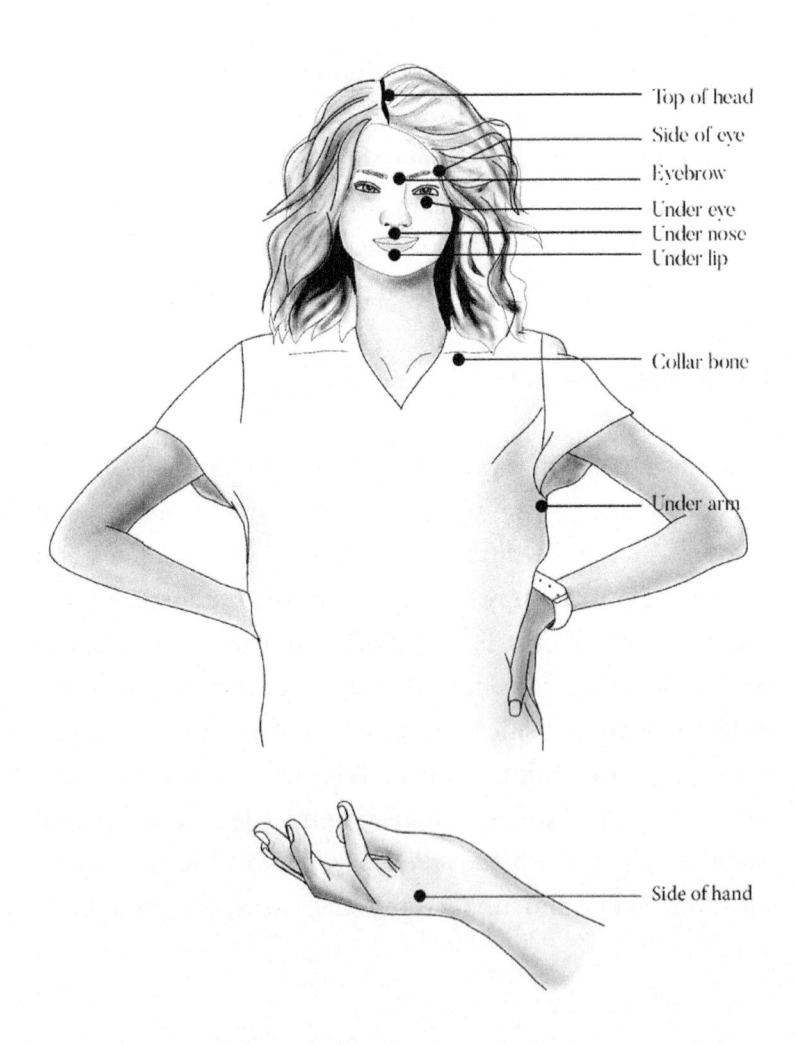

- Top of head
- Side of eye
- Eyebrow
- Under eye
- Under nose
- Under lip
- Collar bone
- Under arm
- Side of hand

Tapping, also referred to as emotional freedom techniques (EFT) utilizes gentle rhythmic tapping at specific points on your body. These specific points are your nine tapping points which are located

- at the crown of your head
- at the outer side of your eye
- at the eyebrow (just above the bridge of your nose)
- under your eye (at the cheekbone)
- under your nose (the philtrum)
- at the indentation below your lip (the labiodental fold)
- at your collarbone point located two points down from your collarbone and towards the collarbones meet
- under your arm
- on the outer edge of your hand (pinky side)

This practice allows us to address and release trauma, emotions, or challenges as tapping stimulates cognitive consciousness and emotional blockages. Tapping stimulates the central nervous system and releases helpful chemicals that aid in reducing stress, managing anxiety, and restoring calm. In tapping, you identify a bothersome feeling, thought, or event, acknowledge these sensations with a statement, and respond with a phrase of acceptance (Bedosky, 2022).

The tapping technique is as follows:

1. Identify and state one problem, emotion, or fear that is on your mind.
2. Rate the intensity of this problem area on a scale from 0 to 10. Assess the intensity of your pain or distress.
3. Establish a statement that identifies your problem area and incorporates a self-acceptance statement, such as, "Even though I have put on weight, I am healthy and beautiful."
4. Meditate on this statement, use one of the nine acupoints, and begin tapping.
5. Repeat your statement as you move on to the next eight tapping points.
6. Continue this process for two to three cycles.
7. At the end of this exercise, rate the intensity of your pain and distress again from 0 to 10. Have your distress levels decreased?
8. If you feel that there is more progress needed, repeat the tapping exercise until you reach a level where you feel at ease.

Progressive Muscle Relaxation

Progressive Muscle Relaxation

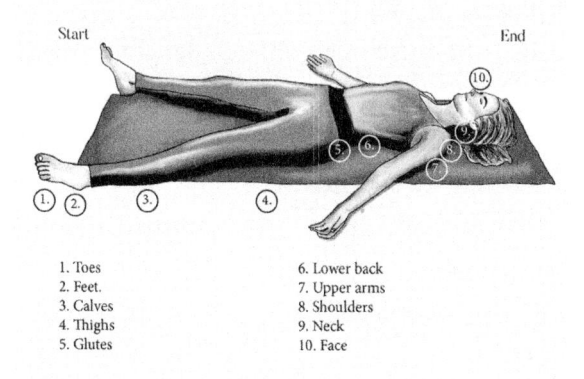

1. Toes
2. Feet
3. Calves
4. Thighs
5. Glutes
6. Lower back
7. Upper arms
8. Shoulders
9. Neck
10. Face

Progressive muscle relaxation (PMR) incorporates tensing and relaxing of the different muscle groups in your body. This exercise decreases high blood pressure, improves sleep, and reduces migraines, anxiety, stress, lower back pain, and muscle tension. It also promotes deep relaxation and improves body awareness. PMR can be incorporated by designating a specific time period and a comfortable setting to practice it, muting digital distractions, wearing lightweight clothing, and beginning at any muscle group area that comes to mind. This exercise is all about being at ease and doing what feels natural.

This is how you can do PMR (Stöppler, 2022):

1. Sit in a comfortable position.
2. For 5 to 10 seconds, inhale and contract one muscle group, such as your feet.
3. Release your muscles as you exhale, picturing stressful feelings or thoughts flowing out of your mind and body.
4. Rest for 10 to 20 seconds.
5. Choose your next muscle group, tense, and inhale for the same amount of time.
6. Exhale and release your muscular tension and troubles.
7. Repeat this exercise for each muscle group you tense.

Body Scan

Mindful body scanning calls for you to silence outside distractions and pay attention to the different parts of your body while taking deep and intentional breaths. Moving from the tip of your toes to the top of your head, you are observing the different feelings and sensations you hold in your body. Body scanning improves sleep, relieves stress and anxiety, reduces pain and unhealthy addictions, and cultivates self-awareness and self-compassion. This practice brings attention to our body and what it needs by fostering an understanding of how it reacts to and stores stress. Body scanning teaches us how to better manage stress and our body's physical reaction to it. As we create a greater mind-body connection, we promote a relaxed state that stimulates healing (Scott, 2024).

You can practice mindful body scanning by

- positioning yourself comfortably
- closing your eyes and focus on your breathing, taking in deep calming breaths
- choosing an area to begin with, such as your feet or your head
- focusing on this area and breathing for 20 seconds to one minute
- repeating this breathing exercise for each spot you're focusing on, working your way through your whole body

As you move from one spot to the next, begin to recognize any pain, tension, or abnormal sensations you are experiencing. If you notice pain and discomfort, acknowledge it, and let your emotions surface. As you inhale and exhale, visualize the pain, tension, discomfort, and negative emotions being released with each breath. Take note of drifting thoughts and gently guide yourself back to the activity and focus on your body. After you have completed a full body scan, become aware of your environment once again, and observe your mental, physical, and emotional relief.

The Role of Mindfulness

Mindfulness teaches us to be aware of our mental and emotional state, and our environment. It aims to improve our focus and concentration by cultivating self-awareness. As you focus on what you feel and identify the root of these feelings, you develop body awareness that brings understanding to your cognitive processing, emotions, and physical feelings.

These are the ways that mindfulness practices enhance body awareness:

- **Try introspection.** Still your mind and your surroundings, take a minute to rest, and evaluate your current emotions. Question your emotions and your thoughts, garnering a deeper understanding of yourself and your reactions.
- **Eat slowly.** Instead of shoveling your food, take a moment to appreciate the different flavors, smells, and textures of your food to cultivate present-moment awareness.
- **Listen to your favorite tunes.** Create a playlist that relaxes and brings you joy to help you unwind and boost your mental and emotional attitude.
- **Blindfold yourself.** Move any delicate or shop objects out of your room. Place a blindfold over your eyes and try to picture what this room looks like. Move or feel your way through the room while trying not to stub your toe. Using your senses, improve your awareness of your surroundings.

- **Live in the moment.** Learn to be spontaneous, be open to new opportunities and adventures, and find joy in the little things.
- **Take meditative walks.** Walk through the park, down a couple of blocks, or on the beach for 10 to 20 minutes. Pay attention to your breathing and your footsteps, the sounds around you, and the sensations in your body.
- **Just breathe.** When we're rushing between tasks, we often forget to breathe. Take a moment to pause and draw your focus inward. Simply be and inhale for 10 deep breaths. This will provide you with levelheadedness and mental clarity before embarking on your next activity.
- **Be intentional.** Decide what your goal is for the day. What do you want to accomplish? What will you not give room to?
- **Have breath awareness.** Take a moment to sit down, engage in deep breathing, and note how this affects your body. Meditate on the sensations in your belly, chest, nostrils, and mouth as you inhale and exhale, and welcome tranquility.
- **Learn to be grounded.** Place your feet flat on the ground, and focus on your breathing and the sensations beneath your feet. As you meditate, inhale and exhale for three seconds each. Grounding is about connecting to nature and becoming in tune with yourself. Learn more about this practice and its healing benefits in the next chapter!

Mind-Body Awareness for Addiction and Recovery

There is a strong association between substance abuse and anxiety, depression, aggression, PTSD, and overwhelming or suppressed negative emotions. When we don't process trauma, it can cause us to disconnect from our bodies, disassociate from our loved ones, and fall into destructive behavior.

When we incorporate body awareness, it can be used to improve and overcome addictions we are facing. The practice of body scanning as a form of active meditation helps those of us who struggle with addiction by bringing awareness and understanding to our body's physical and emotional triggers and signals. This somatic therapy can help us resist temptations, turn away from niggling voices, and prevent us from taking those two steps back.

Training ourselves in mind-body awareness can bring enlightenment and understanding to the way our bodies communicate and guide us on how to give our body what it needs, as opposed to what it wants. The Mindful Awareness in Body-Oriented Therapy (MABT) technique teaches us how to recognize and process the signals our body sends out and helps us to constructively deal with feelings or thoughts that can trigger a relapse (Baumgartner, 2019). Body awareness training decreases symptoms of depression, reduces cravings, and improves emotional regulation, which paves the way for us to engage in self-care practices, and bring our mind and body back into alignment.

Mind-body awareness lends itself to the trauma-informed care approach in treating substance abuse. The trauma-informed care approach acknowledges the many ways trauma can affect your mind, emotions, body, and reality. Using this approach can steady your path to addiction recovery.

By gaining insight into how our brain and autonomic nervous system (ANS) respond to trauma and triggers, we can reduce the physical expressions that ANS overstimulation has on our bodies. These symptoms may be experienced as increased heart rate, hyperventilation, and high stress, often leading us to seek comfort and peace of mind in addictions. Immersing ourselves in our body helps us to understand our current mental and emotional state and how we interact with our environment. Mind-body awareness can help reduce addiction by grounding us in reality, becoming intentional with our healing by acknowledging points of pain and discomfort, and improving our mental and emotional health.

Mirror Work for Negative Body Image

How we perceive our bodies is influenced by our perception of ourselves and the world around us, and our thoughts, feelings, and behavior. Self-perception is guided by the sensations we feel against or within our bodies. Our thoughts are influenced by our cognitive processing, self-beliefs, how we think others see us, and what we interpret our body to be or look like.

How we feel about our bodies contributes to a negative or positive body image. A negative or positive self-perception is governed by the types of thoughts you have toward your body. How loud is the voice of your inner self-critic? How we act is based on a positive or negative body image. Behavior such as sucking in our stomach when we try on a new outfit is a result of poor self-image, body dissatisfaction, or diet culture.

Finding fault with our appearance affects how we see and treat ourselves. Experiencing hypercritical thoughts and giving room to negativity not only affects our self-image, but our ability to trust ourselves, reach our goals, and develop healthy friendships. Examples of negative body image statements are

- I am not beautiful.
- I am worthless.
- No one will love me as I am.

Mirror Work and Exposure

Social media and environment static tell us all kinds of things about what we should be, how we should look, what to eat, and what we need to strive toward as if there is one blueprint to health and happiness. Mirror work is about facing yourself in the mirror, raw and unfiltered. It facilitates a better relationship and appreciation for our bodies and what they have gone through. It teaches us to embrace our body as it is now!

Mirror work is best done with a full-length mirror to observe yourself as a whole. Stand in front of your mirror in either a revealing outfit or nude. Identify areas that cause distressing emotions and take note of how you see yourself. Mirror exposure requires you to face the concerns and criticism you have about your body as you stare into the mirror. This behavioral treatment cultivates a positive body image and fosters self-acceptance and self-respect. Instead of judging, criticizing, or pinching your (perceived) flaws, begin describing the different parts of your body using neutral language. An example of this would be instead of targeting your arms and calling them bat wings, you describe them as gently rounded upper arms. Perhaps you can even associate these physical attributes with someone in your life who you admire and love and who shares these attributes. This may help you see your body in a more positive light. Mirror exposure creates a balanced self-image perspective, improves our relationship with our bodies, and frees us from negative self-thoughts (Jacobs, 2023).

Interactive Element

Body Meditation Scan

Find a period within your day where you can relax and participate in a body scan. This practice can help unwind after a physically and emotionally taxing day or week. In this exercise, you will experience and assess the different thoughts and sensations you are feeling and immerse yourself in them. Kick off this exercise by sitting comfortably and doing a few deep circular breaths. Take note of how you feel at this point and when you're ready, begin your body scan.

1. Start scanning from the top of your head to your feet, and acknowledge areas that are comfortable and uncomfortable.
2. Once you reach your feet, become aware of sensations in this area. When you come across pain or tension, focus on them, and inhale.
3. Acknowledge accompanying thoughts and emotions, visualize them, and release them as you exhale.
4. Scan the rest of your body, continue to give the same attention to each area that carries uncomfortable sensations, and release them.

Body scanning is not relegated to a daytime exercise. In fact, doing this in the evenings works to relax your mind and body, and release the day's tension. Trauma, anxiety, and chronic stress dysregulate cortisol levels and can influence your circadian rhythm. This can lead to disrupted sleep patterns or insomnia. While you're lying in your bed, practicing meditative body scanning can assist with finding restful sleep.

Prompts to Enhance Your Mind-Body Connection

As you scan your body and acknowledge your thoughts and emotions, you are able to develop greater self-understanding and provide clarity on how to move forward. Use the prompts for self-reflection and to enhance your mind-body connection:

- Where do you notice your body stores tension?
- What emotion or event is linked to this physical manifestation?
- What was your main emotion throughout the day? Was it positive or negative?
- What emotions, thoughts, or memories are surfacing right now?
- How do you feel mentally, emotionally, and physically after doing your body scan?

This somatic practice helps us identify how and where trauma affects us and what our triggers are. Having a mind-body awareness guides us to address fears and obstacles, and find ways to manage them. Becoming conscious of ourselves teaches us to be kinder and more compassionate, which facilitates healing and renewal. When we foster a mind-body connection, we can improve and restore our mental, emotional, and physical health.

Incorporating tapping, progressive muscle relaxation, and body scanning can reverse the effects of traumatic or stress-inducing events, and rejuvenate your mind, body, and spirit. As you become aware of your thoughts, emotions, and behaviors, it sheds light on how they affect your social and personal interactions, shape the perception you have of your reality, and how important checking in with yourself is. You are capable of changing how distressing situations affect you. Building a relationship with your mind and body allows you to feel grounded and take control of your thoughts and emotions.

FIVE

Finding Your Ground—The Art of Grounding

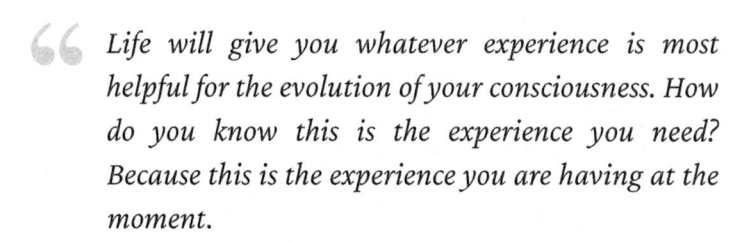

> *Life will give you whatever experience is most helpful for the evolution of your consciousness. How do you know this is the experience you need? Because this is the experience you are having at the moment.*
>
> Eckhart Tolle

Grounding and the Science Behind It

Have you ever stood barefoot in the rain, soaked your feet in the muddy grass, and let the raindrops wash away your sadness and tears? Well, then you may have been unintentionally grounding. This somatic practice incorporates walking barefoot, laying down on a section of grass, weaving your hands through soil, or using grounding devices to build a connection between us and nature. These days you can find grounding mats and patches that work just as well. Grounding theorizes that when we connect our bodies to the Earth's surface, an exchange of positive and negative energy occurs. Absorbing the Earth's natural frequencies brings our body into harmony.

The frequencies from the electronics we use daily and the electromagnetic pollution we are exposed to negatively affect our immune system and energy levels and cause sleep disruptions. Our bodies carry the positive charge and when we come into contact with the Earth's negative charges, the excess positive energy we carry is discharged, and we receive energy in the form of free electrons from the Earth. These free electrons synchronize our bodies to manage the Earth's natural frequencies and aid our overall healing. The Earth's natural frequencies are important to our overall well-being. Grounding can positively influence our body, health, and mood (Gordon, 2023).

The Importance and Benefits of Grounding

Grounding is another form of somatic therapy that not only grounds us in the present but also in the power of nature. This practice is important for cultivating an ideal environment where your mind, body, and spirit can find peace and healing. Grounding can benefit you in the following ways (Gordon, 2023):

- **Improves mood:** Grounding produces a relaxed state and boosts our mood when practiced daily.
- **Enhances quality of life:** Grounding improves energy levels and decreases fatigue. When our energy levels are low and we are overwhelmed and exhausted, we may notice that our ability to function physically decreases and we experience frequent depressive moods, tiredness, and pain. By supporting overall health, grounding can improve these areas.
- **Reduces blood pressure:** Grounding lowers hypertension. Inducing tranquility and a peaceful mental and emotional state, this practice decreases anxiety and stressful thoughts that raise

blood pressure. In a research study of 10 participants who were encouraged to ground, findings reported that their systolic levels decreased by an average of 14.3% by the end of the study period!
- **Improves heart health:** Grounding may improve your cardiovascular health through the application of grounding patches to your hands and feet. These patches provide a flow of electrons to areas with acute or chronic pain, inflammation, or injury. Grounding reduces red blood viscosity and the clumping of red blood cells which decreases the risk of cardiovascular concerns or conditions. High blood pressure, high blood sugar levels, and high frequencies of PTSD increase the risk of cardiovascular disease.
- **Promotes muscle recovery:** The healing capabilities of grounding result in reduced muscle damage and associated pain post-exercise.

Grounding and Trauma Recovery

When we find ourselves triggered and revisiting a traumatic event, we experience intense anxiety, panic attacks, tense muscles, flashbacks, and even disassociation. Grounding helps us find the light when the darkness of vivid traumatic memories and out-of-body experiences closes in. Bringing us into the present, fostering awareness of the feeling of nature around and beneath us, and refocusing our minds and emotions, helps us recover from trauma one step at a time.

Grounding relieves us of a state of physiological arousal, overwhelm, and anxiety. This technique is best implemented when we are hyperactivated, frozen, frightened, hypervigilant, and on edge, or struggling to bring ourselves down from a heightened state. In conjunction with grounding, trauma recovery is enhanced through techniques such as soothing self-talk, meditation, laughing therapy, practicing gratitude, cold water immersion, mindful eating and drinking, and developing present-moment awareness as you walk outside (Khoddam, 2023).

Risks and Safety Precautions

Grounding is largely a safe practice, but precautions need to be taken when deciding where exactly you would like to ground. You need to make sure that the ground you walk or lay upon is not hiding harmful or dangerous objects, insects, or plants, and do prior research on the benefits or dangers of any grounding devices that pique your interest. When you begin grounding, be aware of

- shards of glass hidden between the dirt and blades of glass
- discarded needles at parks
- wasps on the ground
- pollen allergies you may have

If you are pregnant, please think twice before getting down and dirty to reap the benefits of grounding. Soil can contain the contaminant *toxoplasma gondii* which may lead to toxoplasmosis. This could impact the health of your unborn baby by increasing the risk of miscarriages and birth defects (Gordon, 2023).

Grounding Techniques

Grounding seeks to build a mind-body-earth connection to facilitate true healing and build resilience toward negativity. Grounding techniques work to create awareness of ourselves, our emotions, and our environment. Physical, mental, and soothing grounding techniques work to achieve present-moment awareness and build a better relationship with ourselves.

Physical Techniques

Physical techniques make use of our five senses: sight, smell, sound, taste, and touch. Using them allows us to be anchored to our surroundings and become present. These are the grounding techniques that incorporate your body and its senses (Chalica, 2023):

Standing Awareness Exercise

This exercise stimulates present-moment awareness through mindfulness as you learn to be still. This exercise is as follows:

1. Stand as you normally would.
2. Let your hands hang by your sides.
3. Close your eyes and perform a full body scan.
4. Observe and acknowledge what and how you're feeling.

5. Maintain mindfulness, keep your eyes closed, and focus on the sensations within.

Connecting to the Earth

This exercise encourages becoming one with your mind and body and connecting with nature. This improves our ability to be grounded. Connecting to the Earth technique involves

1. Remove your shoes and socks.
2. Stand or sit on a natural surface, such as grass or soil.
3. Close your eyes.
4. Picture a flow of energy being transferred between you and the earth.
5. Breathe deeply and maintain this visualization for five minutes.

Tactile Activation

Tactile activation is a technique that utilizes self-to-self physical contact. Through this process, which uses the sense of touch, our nervous system becomes regulated. This is how tactile activation is conducted:

1. Rub your hands together and warm them up.
2. Place your warm hands on different parts of your body.
3. Take note of the sensations you feel under your hands.
4. Rub your hands together again, reheating them and placing them on a different part of your body.

5. Note new, different, or similar sensations.
6. Repeat this process for any other parts of the body.

Grounding and Centering

This technique takes the exercise of grounding your bare feet to the Earth a little further. For this technique, imagine roots growing from beneath your feet and anchoring themselves into the ground. Complete this exercise by

1. Take your shoes off (if you're comfortable with this).
2. Stand or sit with your feet flat on the ground.
3. Take a few deep breaths and focus on the sensation of your feet connecting with the earth.
4. Visualize roots growing from your feet into the ground.
5. Imagine this is the anchor that connects you to the earth.
6. Shift your weight from left to right and front to back as if you are a tree swaying in the wind.
7. From shifting and swaying, gently bring yourself to a standstill.
8. Bring your awareness to your center of gravity which is located in the upper pelvic area and below the navel.
9. Place your hands above your lower belly, feel your center, and feel how your body is connecting to the earth.
10. Focus on this sensation.

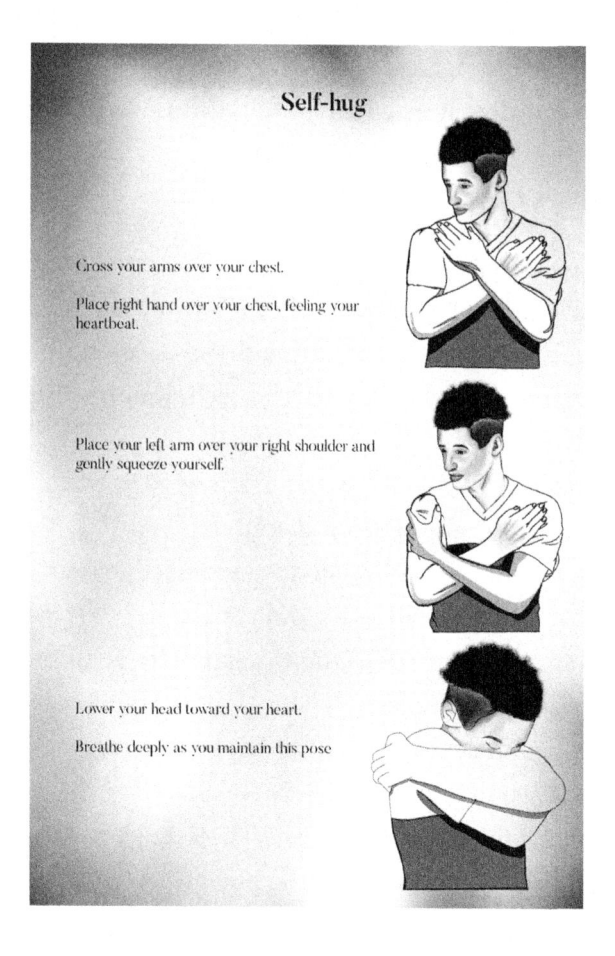

Self-Hug

Self-hug

Cross your arms over your chest.

Place right hand over your chest, feeling your heartbeat.

Place your left arm over your right shoulder and gently squeeze yourself.

Lower your head toward your heart.

Breathe deeply as you maintain this pose

Hugging ourselves can be a soothing and self-comforting gesture when we feel afraid, isolated, or sad. The self-hug promotes a safe and grounded feeling. You can reap the benefits and give yourself a self-hug when you

1. Cross your arms over your chest.
2. Place your right hand over your chest, feeling your heartbeat.

3. Place your left arm over your right shoulder and gently squeeze yourself.
4. Lower your head toward your heart.
5. Breathe deeply as you maintain this pose.

Five Senses Grounding Technique

The exercise is also known as the five-four-three-two-one senses grounding technique. It is a mindfulness exercise that can reduce stress and anxiety through the use of the five senses to bring you back to the present. This technique involves

- using your sense of sight to acknowledge five things you can see around you
- using your sense of touch to acknowledge four things you can touch around you
- using your sense of sound to acknowledge three things you can hear
- using your sense of smell to acknowledge two things you can smell
- using your sense of taste to acknowledge one thing you can taste in your mouth

Mental Techniques

Mental techniques use the concepts of mindfulness, meditation, self-compassion, words of affirmation, and mental stimulation to eliminate or distract from negative and distressing thoughts and replace them with realistic, truth, and positive ones (Raypole, 2024).

Memory Game

Create a game out of an object, painting, or picture you come across. For 5 to 10 seconds study these items and then flip them over or turn away from them. Think about the image of them in your head and try to remember as many details of the object, painting, or picture as possible. To ramp up this game, set a timer for yourself, and test your memory!

Thinking in Categories

Think of one or two unrelated or contrasting categories. Now, try to list all the things you know about each category. For example, if your category was dogs, mentally list all the different breeds you can remember.

Math and Numbers

Similar to counting sheep when trying to nod off, counting can lull us into a sense of ease. For this exercise, run through your favorite timetable or pick a random number and keep adding 25.

Anchoring Statements

Repeating or meditating on statements keeps us focused on what's important, motivates us, and ground us to reality. Anchoring statements can be

- Today is Tuesday the 26th of June.
- I am confident. I am brave.
- I am in control of my emotions.

Visualize

Using your imagination, picture an activity you enjoy doing or will be doing soon. Visualize where you will be doing this task. Think of all the steps you will be taking to complete it. Take note of the sounds and scents associated with this activity.

Soothing Techniques

Soothing techniques focus on bringing calm to your mental and emotional health through positive feelings and thoughts. They focus on people, memories, or objects that create warm and tingly happy sensations in your body (Raypole, 2024).

Picture Someone You Love

When negative or distressing emotions arise, picture the face or voice of someone who brings love and positivity into your life. What would they say? How do they bring you comfort? Let them motivate you through whatever challenges you are navigating.

Practice Self-Kindness

Do you feel as if you're not good enough, can't seem to do anything right, or don't matter? What are the negative thoughts that your inner self-critic is broadcasting? Now, think about the exact opposite of that statement. Turn that criticism into a positive and confidence-boosting statement. Repeat these kind and compassionate phrases to yourself daily (even if you don't believe them just yet).

Pet Therapy

Sit and enjoy quality time with your pet. Think of their quirks and unique character, how they wake you up in the morning, how beautiful their coat is, and the comfort they bring. If you're not at home, think of cherished or humorous moments engraved in your memory.

List Your Favorites

Think of all the things that bring you joy, why they do, and what sensations they evoke. If one of your favorite items is near you, use it, and think about the joy and comfort its presence brings. This can be a cherished blanky, a mug, or a childhood stuffed toy.

Listen to Music

Put on your favorite tunes and let the music move you. Immerse yourself in feelings that arise and lyrics that free your thoughts and emotions. What part of your favorite songs speaks the most to you?

List Positive Things

Think of a handful of items, people, or events that bring you joy, and bring them to the front of your mind. Write down positive things and begin to cultivate gratitude.

Overcoming Challenges in Grounding

Taking a moment to sit with your emotions and thoughts when you'd rather continue avoiding the deeper issues can be a most uncomfortable feeling. Grounding requires us to be still and present, address complicated thoughts and emotions, how our bodies respond to them, and release them. Grounding is not always a natural experience and it can be challenging. These may be the factors standing in the way of fully immersing yourself in grounding.

Physical Distractions

When you are overwhelmed with mental and emotional burdens, exhausted, or plagued by pain, you can become physically uncomfortable. This causes you to hyperfocus on everything that is distressing you and inhibits the ability to be present and aware of your body. As you persevere through the grounding experience and breathe through the discomfort, it won't be long before you find relief and release and learn to present in the moment.

Emotional Discomfort and Overwhelm

Storing and experiencing a wealth of intense emotions can lead to emotional discomfort. A grounding experience can bring up the areas you have dismissed or blanketed and guide you to feeling and expressing them. Having these emotions resurface can be daunting or anxiety-inducing and cause us to shy away from grounding, but when we are not grounded, we become increasingly emotionally vulnerable.

Poor Self-Esteem

Feel broken, unloved, out of place, or that you're not even worth the effort. Perhaps, because of your past, you mistrust the effectiveness of grounding, or you feel as if you are undeserving of the benefits that it can provide. Sometimes, it's easier to hold onto past hurts and self-criticism when we believe them or they have become a familiar crutch. Healing the part of you that feels broken or unloved takes time, and as you connect the Earth and your body, the subconscious resistance to change and hope will lose its power.

Interactive Element

Grounding Anywhere, Anytime

Grounding is not relative to playing in the dirt. There is a greater importance placed on connecting us with nature, anchoring us in the present, releasing negativity, and cultivating peace. When you are experiencing heightened amounts of stress, you don't have to wait until you are at home. There are three grounding techniques that you can use in your office, when you are grocery shopping, or driving.

Grounding Chair

Find a comfortable chair, sit down, press your back against the full support of the chair, and flatten your feet to the ground. Close your eyes and inhale for three counts, then exhale slowly. Focus on your body and how it feels in the chair. Take note of the contact between your body and the chair. Touch the areas of the chair and observe different textures. Push your feet into the ground below and imagine energy draining from the top of your head out to your feet and into the ground below.

Five-Four-Three-Two-One

Stimulate your five senses and increase your awareness of movement, changes, and sensations around you. Sit comfortably, close your eyes, inhale through your nose for three counts, and exhale slowly through your mouth for the same amount of time. Now, you're ready to begin! (See the Five Senses Grounding Technique above.)

Hold an Object

Look around your home or office for an object that catches your eye, has texture, or has an odd design. Hold it in your hand and focus on its appearance. Observe the different colors, patterns, or finish that it has. Acknowledge the weight of it in your hand and how the shadows fall on it as you shift it around. This exercise can be done with precious stones, small sculptures, and snow globes.

Prompts to Reflect on During Grounding

As you focus on the object in your hand, it is a good time to self-reflect. Take this period of tranquility and mental hush to answer the following prompts:

- What brings you joy?
- What kind of weather do you enjoy?

- What is the sound that brings you comfort when you are still?
- What message do you have for your younger self?
- What are three things you appreciate about your adult self?

When we are not grounded, we can feel disconnected from our loved ones, our emotions, and our reality. The practice of grounding enhances the mind-body connection by improving our awareness and extending it to nature. Connecting our mind and body to the earth and our surrounding nature improves our ability to tackle uncomfortable emotions, confront the negative feelings we have about ourselves, and allow our bodies to heal and regulate themselves.

The art of grounding teaches how to push through uncomfortable emotions and negative thoughts and incorporate techniques that not only cultivate present-moment awareness but positivity as well. Grounding techniques are important for managing distressing thoughts, emotions, and memories. When trauma resurfaces, it can lead to abnormal system functions, such as altering the way we are able to think, act, breathe, and function. Grounding techniques improve our resilience to manage and bounce back when trauma induces these foreign reactions.

From Surviving to Thriving

"Forgetting was not the same as healing."

Rivers Solomon

There are an incredible number of people living in survival mode without even realizing it. Life never lets up: We run from one thing to the next with barely a moment to catch our breath and reflect on the things that have hurt us. The longer that goes on, the more it affects us, and the harder it is to access the peace and joy that life has to offer.

There has never been more of a need for somatic therapy: Our minds and bodies are under constant stress, and our bodies carry any element of trauma that hasn't been addressed, constantly adding to the strain we're under. It doesn't have to be this way, and somatic therapy offers us an alternative. The problem is, not enough people know how to implement it.

This book is designed to change that, empowering you with the tools you need to release your pain and improve your mental, physical, and emotional wellness... and you can help other people access those tools.

By leaving a review of this book on Amazon, you'll help other people find the gateway to somatic therapy and discover just how realistic it is for them to spark the changes they're looking for.

Awareness about somatic therapy is growing, and people are searching for advice on how to use it. Your review will help them find it.

Thank you so much for your support. Healing is a personal journey, but the support of others is crucial, and you're making an incredible difference by taking a moment to share this wisdom.

SIX

The Dance of Recovery— Understanding Pendulation

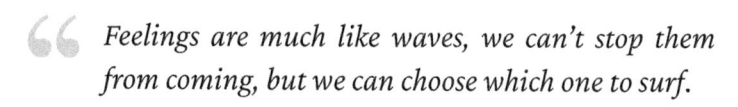

> *Feelings are much like waves, we can't stop them from coming, but we can choose which one to surf.*
>
> Jonatan Mårtensson

Pendulation Explained

Pendulation takes us back and forth between a whirlpool of trauma and one of healing. This therapeutic approach moves us between distressing, traumatic, and fearful memories and memories that hold joy, love, hope, and positivity. Moving between these two opposing areas enables us to self-regulate by decreasing the effect negativity may have on us, improving emotional intelligence, and building mental and emotional resilience. As we are moved between a trauma whirlpool and a healing whirlpool, we are able to titrate the recall of stressful events (Levine, 2010).

By cultivating this balance, the hold past trauma has had on our self-perceptions, mental and emotional health, and our body decreases. The looping process of pendulation allows trauma in the form of frozen energy to be released and, with it, physical pain, panic attacks, and insomnia. Pendulation allows the body to overcome the physical manifestations of unprocessed trauma and allows the body's systems to be regulated and work in balance.

How Pendulation Works

Pendulation focuses on the intimate and sensitive connection between the mind and the body. As we are gently swinging from two contrasting states and experience uncomfortable emotions, we learn to tolerate them, break them down, and gradually release them (Sabater, 2023). Traumatic experiences cause the central nervous system to immobilize us and allow the effects of trauma to manifest physically. Pendulation stimulates the central nervous system to decrease the intensity of psychological trauma. It takes us from a heightened state, cultivates a sense of calm, and trains our mind and brain to confront negative past experiences.

The process of pendulation is experienced when a trigger response places us in an acute distressing state. When a trigger response leads to stress, overwhelm, and increased anxiety, we need to observe and acknowledge how this affects us physically. This helps us become cognizant of any area on our body that holds distress. Think about how these areas make you feel. Focus on these areas and describe the sensations. Engage with these sensations and conduct a full body scan to identify any area that feels neutral or pain-free. Take note if less distress is felt in these areas. Question if these areas are free from emotional pain.

Experiencing and exploring these neutral areas allows you to become familiar with them and articulate what it feels like. Gradually and gently, we will shift back and forth between areas that hold distress and tension and the areas that are pain-free. The practice of pendulating between these two areas will continue until the distressed areas on our body find ease.

The Benefits and Importance of Pendulation

As pendulation takes place and creates homeostasis in the body by releasing stored psychological trauma, the benefits of this process exceed just the physical. Regulating the central nervous system aids our body in reconnecting with our mind and body, improving awareness, and fostering healthier relationships with ourselves and our loved ones. These are the many ways that pendulation can bring improvements (Hanson, 2014):

- **Embodiment:** Cultivating being present in our bodies creates a deeper understanding and awareness of the body and who we are.
- **Learning to be an observer of self:** Pendulation develops the ability to remain a neutral observer in states of chaos or emotional extremes.

- **Becoming aware of the unconscious:** We are able to become conscious of our unconscious cognitive processing and behavior.
- **Interconnectivity of our inner states:** Pendulation highlights that we have many complex inner states that exist and work together.
- **Self-connection:** The development of a connection with ourselves and an inner connectivity between parts of self takes place.
- **Finding positivity:** Trauma can keep us locked in a state of fearfulness and negativity. Pendulation teaches that not only can we hold positivity, goodness, peace, and wholeness in our many inner states, but that our surrounding worlds contain these treasures as well.
- **Seeing resources:** Through pendulation, we learn to identify internal and external resources.
- **Receive resources:** Pendulation teaches us to open up to, be receptive to, connect with, and receive benefits from those resources.
- **Self-regulation:** We are able to build self-regulation, which reduces how our mind and body respond to distress.
- **Empowerment:** We learn that we are in control of our emotions and physiological state and that we can manage how our body is activated.
- **Nervous system flexibility:** Our nervous system's natural flexibility is restored through pendulation which releases us from an activated, frozen, and immobile state.

- **Decreasing feelings of overwhelm:** Pendulation encourages the transition from feelings of never-ending pain, fear, or anxiety to a state where these experiences become finite and manageable.
- **Restoring our inner child:** For some of us feeling safe, loved, and protected was part of our childhood. As a result, this becomes our internal working model of attachment. Pendulations help us reconnect with these memories and feelings. During this technique, when you begin to feel that child-like wonder, curiosity, trust, and hope, pendulation and restoration are at work! Through this process, we are able to move on from fear, anxiety, dread, and hopelessness, and find safety and security.

Navigating Emotional Waves

When we are overwhelmed and find ourselves filled with despair, we are accompanied by emotions such as anxiety, depression, sadness, anguish, and desperation. Perhaps you want things to change or are hoping that someone else can take all the pain away. The emotions you associate with these moments can feel all-consuming and like waves that just keep on coming. It's truly a wonder that you've managed to keep your head above water for this long. Although emotional waves feel as if there is no end in sight, there is a way to navigate it all.

Emotional waves have a beginning, a middle, and an end. When the first few emotions surface, they do not seem as threatening, but the longer we suppress them, the greater they become. Emotions feel intense when they climb to overwhelming heights in the middle, but they will soon break and recede. This middle part is known as the high distress zone. At this point, you may have racing thoughts that may be extreme, it may seem as if you've lost time, you are haunted by fears of death or a loss of control, you may feel disconnected from the present, and you may experience strong uncomfortable physical sensations.

Like the ocean, there is an ebb and flow, and eventually, all that overwhelm will come to pass. Science has shown that we can build up and process our emotions in 90 seconds (Tomasello, 2021). The 90-second rule states that if you feel emotions bubbling, experience them and let them run their course. Develop an understanding of the root of these emotions, what may have triggered them, and how they make you feel. After the 90 seconds, engage in an activity to shake off any lingering negative effects.

There is no control when it comes to waves in the ocean and similarly, you cannot control the waves of emotions coming your way. Someway and somehow, you're going to have to learn to surf. Accept that you cannot control how you feel in situations. We need to learn how to manage and process our feelings in a healthy way. It's best to simply let our emotions out. What we resist, will eventually become persistent. The more we try to control or suppress our emotions, the more emotionally vulnerable and unstable we may become. Emotions eventually find their way to the surface. Let's facilitate a healthy way for them to come up, instead of letting them overwhelm us in one big tidal wave.

Learning to ride the wave means sitting through emotional waves. To learn to surf the wave, we need to spot triggers or become sensitive to when our emotional state and mood take a turn. Just like when we take note of rip currents at the beach, spotting an incoming emotional wave is important. Observe how you feel and name the emotions. Is it anxiety, calm, or rage that you are experiencing? Bring awareness to why these emotions have sprung up. What thoughts are connected to this experience? Is there an area you have not found closure in yet? Perhaps, you are holding a grudge? Making it through emotional waves requires us to be open and honest with ourselves. Changing and healing our mindset works as breakwaters that protect us from devastating and overwhelming emotional waves (Cenizal, 2022).

The Therapeutic Process of Pendulation

There is harmony in the coming together of opposites. The duality of yin and yang, the negative energy of the earth and our positive energy, speaks of how the culmination of opposites brings harmony and balance. Pendulation utilizes the concept of opposing ends, i.e., a state of distress and a state of calm to guide our body into releasing emotional and physical tension. When we release them, we are able to cultivate ease and balance within and around ourselves.

Somatic pendulation therapy incorporates mindful steps that help us connect with experiences of distress, fear, and anxiety and experiences of calm, joy, and happiness. This is how you can practice pendulation:

1. When you feel distressed, take a moment to tune into your body and build awareness.
2. Identify the physical sensations within your body that are related to your current emotional state.
3. Acknowledge these areas, concentrate on them, and feel them.
4. Scan your body for an area that is without pain and distress, i.e., neutral and calm areas. These areas may be experiencing less pain as well.
5. What are the sensations in this area? Meditate on this area of your body for a few moments.
6. If you are struggling to find a neutral area, make use of an external object as the source of your serenity. Use this object as an anchor.
7. You can conjure up imagery or memories that encapsulate distressing emotions.
8. Pendulate (swing) between distressing memories and your calming object.
9. When the negative sensations seem overwhelming, gently pivot back to the object.
10. Pendulate between the negative and the positive areas rhythmically, until how you experience and are affected by the distressing emotions transforms.

The Role of Pandulation in Emotional Regulation

Don't worry, this is not a typo. Pandulation predates the conception and theorization of pendulation. Rooted in biology and somatic practices, it utilizes the body to stretch, contract, and yawn our reflexes to release accumulated muscular tension and promote relaxation. Our psychological state affects our bodies in the form of pain, tension, and fatigue. Our emotional state is affected by the physical effects of trauma and can also be the cause of it. Practicing pandulation not only restores physical imbalances and tension but helps regulate our emotional state.

Pandulation is an exercise that can be done in most settings. Follow these steps to incorporate this exercise in the comfort of your home (Audice Wellness Services, 2023):

1. **Build awareness and intention:** Designate a time and space where you are unlikely to be disturbed. Focus on your body and take note of the different sensations you feel. Become aware of your current emotional state. If you experience any emotional or physical tension or discomfort, make a note of this observation. Intentionally release this tension and create a relaxed and harmonious emotional, physical, and emotional state.
2. **Gentle movement and stretching:** Gently move and stretch your body until you feel your body awaken. You can do this by rolling your shoulders, rotating your neck, and lifting your arms above and over your head. This works to unwind knots and tight sensations within your body, increase your flexibility, and invigorate you.
3. **Contract and release:** Focus on a muscle group and contract this area gently. Maintain this contraction for five counts. Slowly release the muscle until it is fully relaxed. As you repeat this

intentional exercise for specific or tension-filled muscle groups, you will feel your body slowly release any tension as you relax your muscles.

4. **Mindful breathing:** As you shift between distressing and neutral areas, inhale deeply through your nose and exhale slowly through your mouth. This mindful breathing exercise promotes relaxation and emotional awareness as it connects our body with our emotions. Controlled and cyclical breathing can slowly bring you down from a heightened state and lull you into a calm.

5. **Reflect and observe:** After you contract and release a muscle group, completing a cycle, reflect on the sensations you are experiencing. Observe and acknowledge how your body has shifted from a pained and uncomfortable state to one that is relaxed and calm. Observe and acknowledge the changes you are feeling.

Benefits of Pandulation for Emotional Well-Being

Pandulation helps us to manage and express our pent-up emotions. As we contract and release our muscles, we can unlock the many ways pandulation improves our emotional well-being. These are the benefits of pandulation (Audice Wellness Services, 2023):

- **Reduces stress:** Pandulation combines muscle engagement and relaxation that stimulates our body's parasympathetic nervous system and activates the rest and digest response. This allows us to foster calm and reduce stress levels.

- **Integrates mind and body:** Health and healing through pandulation is cultivated by integrating our physical sensations and emotional states. Pandulation promotes self-awareness and a deeper understanding of how emotions manifest in our bodies.
- **Enhances mindfulness:** Becoming aware of sensations in our body and our emotions, heightens our ability to be mindful and be present.
- **Regulates emotions:** Improving the mind-body connection brings understanding to and regulates our emotional responses. Mindfulness helps us understand the relationship between the physical tension we experience and our emotional responses.
- **Empowerment and self-care:** As we incorporate this technique, we learn to take an active role in managing our emotions and response to trauma to improve our emotional well-being as a form of self-care.

Interactive Element

Pendulate at Home

It's time to teach overwhelming thoughts and emotions who is actually in control. Create a calming space on your bedroom floor or in your living room. Create a quiet atmosphere and limit outside and digital disturbances. If you would like to improve this somatic experience, draw your curtains or light a candle. Perhaps, a candle with your favorite sense can even be your positive object that brings you peace and back into the present.

Let's start this pendulation exercise by doing a few stretches. Place both your mind and body at ease. Do a few circular breaths and when you're ready, follow the instructions below:

1. Think back to an event that caused you great physical and mental distress. It can be a time that someone publicly embarrassed you or belittled you. Maybe it was a period when you felt abandoned or neglected by those you trusted.
2. Hold this memory. What emotions are surfacing right now? How is this affecting you physically?
3. Welcome and immerse yourself in these emotions and sensations. Let them be amplified.
4. Now, think of a new positive memory. Think among these of joy, positivity, love, happiness, laughter, and warmth. What memory comes to mind?
5. Acknowledge the physical, mental, and emotional sensations this kinder memory evokes.
6. Let these happy thoughts and feelings consume you.
7. Gently move between the strong yet opposing memories.

8. Move between the negative and positive sides until you are no longer bowled over by distressing emotions and are able to regulate your breathing and physical expressions throughout the pendulation.
9. Once you have succeeded, take a few deep calming breaths.

Introspective Post-Pendulation Prompts

As you complete the at-home pendulation exercise, take a moment to simply be present and enjoy this sense of accomplishment. You are another step closer to becoming stronger and taking back control of your mental, emotional, and physical well-being. When you have completed pendulating, use these prompts to strengthen your self-understanding and self-awareness:

- Think back to your younger self. What are three things that they would love about your current self or be proud of?
- Remember a time when you were faced with something challenging and overcame it. What was it?
- What does success mean to you?
- Write about the place where you grew up. How has it shaped you?
- What is your earliest childhood memory?

Learning to overcome intense emotions and heightened states of arousal, lies in our ability to gain control of our mind and emotions. This is not easy, especially when we feel exhausted and broken. When we are feeling low in spirit, motivation, and positivity, it becomes increasingly challenging to stand up tall and take charge. This is why pendulation is so important! It helps us manage negative emotions and memories, which makes room for positive influences in our lives. Bridging an understanding between our mind and our body helps us to manage our emotions better and build resilience toward future distressing experiences.

SEVEN

Building Resilience—The Power of Resourcing

> *Resilience is accepting your new reality, even if it's less good than the one you had before. You can fight it, you can do nothing but scream about what you've lost, or you can accept that and try to put together something that's good.*
>
> Elizabeth Edwards

What Is Resourcing?

Resourcing refers to the identified and instilled skills that can help us manage stress, anxiety, distress, and triggers that bring past traumatic experiences to the forefront of our minds. This practice focuses on resolving complex reactions to trauma, such as fear-inducing memories, disturbing thoughts and images, and bodily sensations. Resourcing allows us to face traumatic memories and facilitate physiological stabilization by adopting and utilizing calming tools and skills and encouraging present-moment awareness.

Resourcing is separated into two forms of resourcing: internal and external. *Internal resourcing* is when we are able to recognize the onset of bodily changes and emotional reactions to threats in our vicinity due to past traumatic experiences. In response to this identification and acknowledgment, we may respond by taking a more relaxed response, calming our breathing, and trying to find mental clarity as a form of taking control of the situation. Internal resourcing relies on altering our internal systems to prevent moving to a state of extreme stress or anxiety. *External resourcing* is the use of activities that further promote a rest and digest state. Have you ever been in an overly anxious state and decided to either bake or go swimming to distract yourself and work off frantic energy? That is a form of external resourcing. Additional activities can be yoga, knitting, mindful walking, talking to a friend, or any constructive activity that improves your mental, emotional, and physical well-being.

How Does It Work?

There is a process to developing self-resourcing and identifying the skills and techniques that best work as your coping mechanism. In resourcing, we work to find the most tolerable window that allows you to process and focus on self-regulating and calming your system. Your window of tolerance is where your mind and body are connected and you are able to face distressing memories without experiencing intense emotion, freezing, or disassociating. To get to this place we need to bring attention to our red zones and become desensitized to it.

The red zone is the area where traumatic memories arise and we are unable to process overwhelming emotions and toxic stress. This stress imprints on our brain and body, making us feel trapped in our memories and emotions. Resourcing works to recover energies that are stuck and memories that are lost in order to bring back feelings of wholeness and positivity and regulate the autonomic nervous system (ANS). When we simply exist instead of living and thriving, our ANS places us in a state of survival and ignites fight, flight, and freeze responses to stay highly activated. Resourcing allows us to move into the blue zone —the area where we are able to tolerate past experiences and memories and bring peace and healing to our whole being.

In resource therapy, you are asked to focus on an object that catches your attention. As you focus on this object, think about how it makes you feel and what thoughts or attributes come to mind as you stare at it. When we observe an object that piques our interest or that we delight in, we often use positive descriptive language. As you answer the questions relating to the object, think about the last time you described yourself in such a way. Can you remember the last time you described or perceived yourself as beautiful, lovely, or valuable?

Meditate on and express how these questions make you feel. Do you find yourself moving into the red zone where you are overwhelmed or experiencing negative emotions, such as denial of such a truth? Perhaps you do not believe you are attractive and you have a negative sense of self. Do you move into the blue zone where you accept and welcome this as the truth? Maybe you find yourself somewhere in between, such as the purple zone. An area where you tolerate a semblance of truth but the thought makes you a bit uncomfortable.

Overtime resource therapy allows you to move past negative thoughts and memories, decrease your sensitization to trauma-related cognitive processing and emotions, find and develop your areas of strength, and cultivate resources that provide you with safety, security, and joy.

The Four Es of Resource Therapy

Resourcing is any activity that takes you from the red zone to the blue zone and improves your window of tolerance. What resource works for one does not necessarily work for another. A resource is not universally thought of as a healthy or positive activity. It all depends on where your strengths and challenges lie. Let's take the resource of self-isolation. For someone who struggles with boundaries, always finds themselves doing the most for everyone else to their own detriment, and is constantly being drained by others, isolation as a resource is healthy for them. This allows them to prioritize themselves and practice self-care.

Resourcing is about the prioritization of safety, rather than the desire for social connections and acceptance. Resource therapy looks at your areas that are overdeveloped and those that are underdeveloped through a gentle nonviolent approach to create conditions for transformation. Self-awareness of past resources and patterns and new resources that prove beneficial are developed through exploring, expanding, experiencing and experimenting, and further expanding.

The First E: Exploring

Bring your current challenge to the forefront of your mind. What effect does this have on your body? Do you notice any patterns in what you observe and experience? As you describe events and experiences, take note of what you are good at and where you struggle. In resourcing, you will observe and assess your strengths and weaknesses through probing questions or guesses, such as "It seems like you're good at accomplishing what you set out to do," and present an activity in which to display your natural ability in this area. This demonstrates genuine curiosity throughout resourcing and brings enlightenment to our subconscious thoughts, practices, and capabilities.

The Second E: Expanding the Overdeveloped

Exploring brought awareness to areas where we shine and where we fall short. Expanding focuses on bringing greater awareness to these areas and showcasing the many choices we have. We learn to expand and improve where our strengths lie as we rely on these positive attributes to anchor us in the present and build resilience against negativity.

The Third E: Experiencing and Experimenting

Through activities, we are able to improve our mindfulness and reflect on what we observe about ourselves and whether we notice patterns in our behavior and thinking. In this experiment, our curiosity builds as we highlight subconscious patterns and what they are rooted in. Through this process, question the sensations you feel right now to cultivate present-moment awareness.

The Fourth E: Expanding the New

As you travail your subconscious mind and discover new information about yourself, explore this new awareness, build curiosity, and expand on the newness.

Why Resourcing Is Essential

Think of resourcing a toolbox that holds essential life tools within our brains. When you need it, all you have to do is access your toolbox, and it will have just what you need to foster support, strength, and security. Resources help us digest traumatic activation and provide us with the ability to handle life. These tools and skills we acquire allow us to create a space that has more room for positivity and no longer allows trauma to captivate all areas of our lives. As we learn and adopt more resourcing while our bodies and minds are not activated, that knowledge is stored in our brains, and when we are triggered, we can access it and douse the flame before it roars to life. Resourcing allows us

- to rewire traumatized brains.
- to build trust within our bodies.
- to feel good.
- to achieve our goals.
- to live a passionate life.
- to work smarter, instead of harder.

Self-Resourcing

Self-resourcing is a way of emotional, physical, and mental regulation that can help build confidence and reinforce a sense of inner strength or control over yourself and your life. And let's be honest, most of us might like to feel a little more in control sometimes. Feeling confident in your ability to manage your experience despite environmental factors can be an important asset when it comes to moving you through challenges, and it can also help allow you to access the awareness to ask for help when you're experiencing something that doesn't need to be managed alone.

When to Self-Resource

Self-resourcing allows us to find and apply resources within ourselves that can regulate our emotions, physical reactions, and mental state. When we do this, we are finding and fortifying our inner strength. Through self-resourcing, we can display greater control over our emotional reactions to trauma and stress and are able to overcome negative experiences.

Through finding inner resources, we build confidence and learn to trust ourselves as we improve our awareness and learn to lean on others for support. Self-resourcing can help you manage heightened stress, periods of transition, and great changes when you experience a new relationship or the breakdown of one. Self-resourcing is especially beneficial when we feen unsafe, threatened, in distress, or several other stressors that impact our overall health.

Steps on How to Practice Self-Resourcing

When our minds are in a stressed state, we are overwhelmed by strong emotions, our inner self-critic is amplified, and we are sensitive to environmental static, it can be hard to find resources within ourselves. Self-resourcing requires us to find our inner strength and build our confidence and trust in ourselves, which can be difficult when we fail to recognize the goodness within. We need to practice mindfulness and improve our self-awareness if we want to self-resource to the best of our abilities! Follow these steps to learn how to be a resource for yourself (Redman, 2021; Zapata, 2021):

- Become attuned to your nervous system. Observe and acknowledge when your body begins to shift to a fight, flight, or frozen state and when it begins to disassociate. Think of positive memories and what brings you peace of mind. Implement that exercise or practice and come back to the present. File this inner resource into your toolbox!

- Find out what exercises or practices bring you peace, release stuck energies and emotions, and improve your resilience to negativity. Become attuned to your body, notice what feels good, and incorporate it into your daily life.
- Take a moment to still your mind and become mindful during heightened experiences. What is your body telling you? Pay attention to your inner wisdom and let it guide your decisions.
- Bring positivity and joy into your environment by learning to enjoy what you do, where you are, and even what you are eating. Listen to music that invigorates you or soothes your mind, and engage with nature.
- When you are feeling down, boost your mood by reminding yourself of your strengths, accomplishments, self-affirmations, and happy memories. This will motivate you to move forward.
- Practice the external resource of yoga to improve internal resources such as our intuition, inner strength, and our ability to self-regulate.

To further develop your inner resources, you can observe and listen to those around you. Consider the coping mechanisms they employ and see if they work for you. Change your mindset from believing that spending time thinking and observing is a waste of time. These moments of solitude are pivotal to self-reflect and better understand ourselves. They guide us to cultivate empathy and compassion, not only for ourselves but for others as well. The people we surround ourselves with are important to how we self-resource. Surrounding yourself with emotionally strong people guides you to adopt their way of thinking and behaving to improve yourself. Self-resourcing also means to ask for help when you need it. You don't have to struggle or muddle through life on your own. Rely on these friendships for support and encouragement on how to manage challenging periods (Jacobson, 2023).

Cultivating Resources

When it comes to inner resources, we are motivated by the need for safety, finding satisfaction, and building connections. Resourcing feeds these areas which allow us to navigate stress and create the space for personal growth. To fully cultivate resources, we have to do a deep dive into our conscious and subconscious minds and develop a greater understanding of who we are and what we are capable of. Acknowledge a challenge you commonly find yourself facing. Is there an inner resource that can help you through this period? Can you develop this resource and internalize this experience? Use these steps below to further cultivate your resources and improve your well-being.

1. Identify and affirm what you are good at.
2. Redirect your thoughts to ones that are positive, healthy, or encouraging when negative thoughts arise.
3. When you struggle to see results or the end of the road, remind yourself of how far you've come, the hurdles you've overcome, and your inner strength.

4. Set reasonable goals and achieve them. Celebrate the small and big accomplishments.
5. Lean on and find support from people who want to see you succeed.
6. Incorporate laughter and joy in your life. Good humor and not self-deprecating humor.

Interactive Element

Personal Resource Mapping Activity

Today, you're going to embark on a journey to discover and map your personal resources. These are the tools, practices, and supports that help you navigate through life, especially during challenging times. This process is rooted in somatic therapy, which emphasizes the connection between the mind and body.

Step 1: Identifying Your Resources

First, let's identify your resources. These can be anything that brings you comfort, strength, or a sense of peace. They might be internal, like a positive memory or a physical sensation that calms you, or external such as a supportive friend or a favorite place.

- **Internal resources:** Do a body scan and focus on an area that feels calm or relaxed. What emotions are you associating with this feeling? Is it contentment, calm, or happiness? Observe your body's physical changes as you meditate on these

emotions. Can you feel your body relaxing tense muscles, your rapid breath rate decreasing, and your churning stomach being soothed?
- **External resources:** Consider the people, places, and activities that support you. This could include friends, family, therapists, a peaceful spot in nature, or activities like yoga or painting. What emotions are evoked as you visualize them? Do you feel safe, loved, and accepted? As these emotions become a balm to your soul, do you feel more at peace or confident? Can you notice an ease within your body taking place?
- Take a few moments to write down these resources. Be as specific as possible.

Step 2: Creating Your Resource Map

Now, let's create a visual map. You can draw this on paper, create a digital version, or simply visualize it in your mind.

- **Draw a circle:** In the center, write "Me." This represents you at your core.
- **Add branches:** From this circle, draw branches out into smaller circles or shapes. Each of these represents a different resource.
- **Label each resource:** Write down what each resource is. For internal resources, you might draw a heart or a brain; for external resources, you might draw a symbol that represents that person, place, or activity.

Step 3: Connecting Resources With Feelings

Next to each resource, write down how it makes you feel or how it helps you. For example, next to a friend's name, you might write "understood" or "safe."

Step 4: Accessing Your Resources

Reflect on how you can access these resources.

Ask yourself

- How can I remind myself of these resources when I'm feeling low?
- Are there any barriers to accessing these resources, and how can I overcome them?

Step 5: Regular Review

Finally, make it a habit to review and update your resource map regularly. As you grow and change, your resources might also evolve.

This image is an example of Emily's resource map. Use this as a guide to establish your own resource map, which you can do by scanning the QR code below!

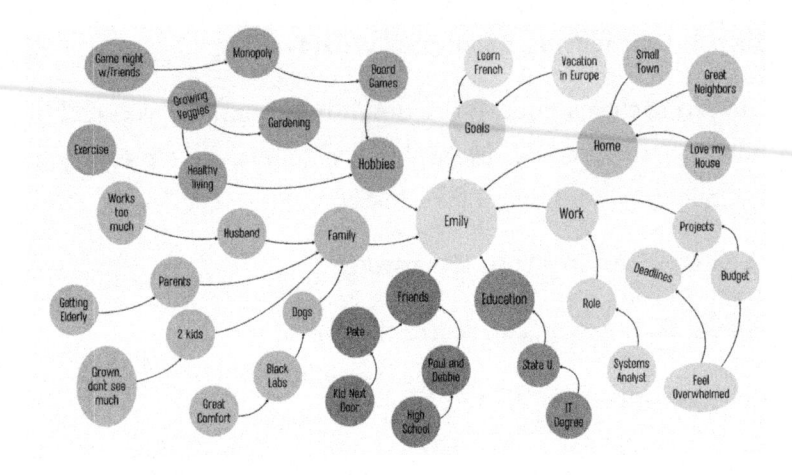

Resourcing is a compact set of tools and skills that you can find and grow within yourself and acquire through external resources. Internal and external resources cultivate internal strength, calm, resilience, and confidence within who we are and what we can achieve. This somatic practice not only deepens our mind-body connection but fosters a greater relationship with ourselves.

Resourcing increases happiness, strengthens relationships, helps us manage problems, and reduces stress. Through resourcing, we can accomplish our goals, improve our work performance, and cultivate satisfaction and purpose in our lives. Learn to be in tune with your body and discover your inner strength. Resourcing is essential to combatting minor and major stressors so that we are no longer fazed by life's challenges. Each time we are exposed to stressful situations, we will be able to bring ourselves back to the present and take control of our emotional, mental, and physical state, one step at a time.

EIGHT

The Art of Control—Mastering Titration

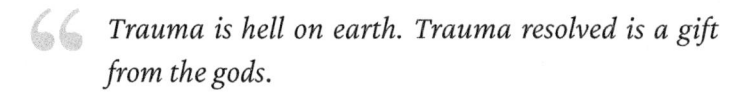

> *Trauma is hell on earth. Trauma resolved is a gift from the gods.*
>
> Peter A. Levine

Understanding Titration

If you're familiar with chemistry, you know that *titration* is the chemical process that occurs when a titrant is slowly dripped into a solution until neutralization and transformation take place. Somatic transformation is the gradual process of neutralizing and transforming our physiological response to trauma. Under this process, we are exposed to small amounts of trauma at a time to build tolerance and resilience. In this manner, we are no longer overwhelmed by strong sensations and heightened emotions. Instead, we can overcome negative experiences one small step at a time.

Titration essentially means slowly working through difficult experiences and managing how quickly we process things. You learn to pace yourself and deal with one minuscule trauma-related aspect, overcome it, and build resilience until you move on to the next small area. As you pay attention to the sensations you experience when revisiting trauma, you will learn to be less affected by them. With each step in titration, we are fostering healing and wholeness in the areas that we tackle.

Slowing, Portioning, and Re-Traumatization

In the process of titration, we make use of resourcing and pendulation to improve our reaction to trauma and triggers. Resourcing allows us to address dark thoughts and memories, using happy memories and calming actions to combat the negative overwhelming feelings that traumatic thoughts and memories may bring. Resourcing is the lifeline that brings us back from the dark abyss of our minds and into our current reality. Pendulation is the process of moving between states of trauma and harmony to create a resilient nervous system and mental and emotional health. Pendulation proves effective as we incorporate resources to create balance in our bodies and regain control of our emotional expression.

Titration helps us reach the aforementioned states of well-being by addressing trauma in small increments. This process utilizes the practices of slowing and portioning to bring harmony to our nervous system. Trauma and reliving traumatic memories can feel as if your boat is taking on too much water and you're sinking. Trauma tends to come at us swiftly and does not give us a chance to breathe or see the light. These experiences lead to overwhelming and suffocating sensations and emotions.

To ensure that we are not subject to these high-stress-inducing sensations and situations, we use methods that are the very opposite of them. In slowing and portioning, you are able to direct just how many distressing emotions and memories resurface. You can choose which trauma areas to address and work through now, and which ones to store away for a time when you have the mental and emotional capacity to deal with them.

When you feel triggered, or trauma is resurfacing, and the associated sensations and emotions are about to bowl you over, call upon your resources and slow down your emotional and physical expressions. Take it all the way down until you have reached a semblance of normalcy and calm. The slow practice of titration helps us manage the way our body processes thoughts and emotions by becoming aware of them.

Now, let's take time to evaluate what triggered the response and what memories arose as a result. Instead of looking at or experiencing an entire traumatic event again, focus on a specific memory or area of the event. This is where the portioning section comes in. Highlight one small area and work on this memory until you can set it free and subsequently release yourself from it. Doing this allows you to be less affected by that specific traumatic event. Slowing and portioning help chip away at an impenetrable dark force, until its strength and armor wanes.

As you focus on each tiny portion, one step at a time, and work through it slowly, you are allowing yourself to heal on a deeper and more permanent level. Working on small bits of difficult memories allows us to move from a defensive and threatened state to one that is protective (Hanson, 2016). As the director of your memory box and emotional state, you are putting a stop to overwhelming waves of emotions that stun your body. Titration can be seen as a protective and resilience-building process that lets you unravel and eliminate traumatic memories one bit at a time and in a safe, controlled environment.

Slowing and portioning allow you to prioritize your emotions and how they affect you in this area of trauma. Titration allows you to listen to your emotions and your body and seek to understand its reaction to trauma. It allows you to separate coupled emotions and linked events, and deal with each one on its own. In this process, you are making room for your emotions and your body to express itself and halt re-traumatization.

With trauma, it can feel as if too much is happening too fast (Hanson, 2016). Titrations seek to heal by reversing the way trauma overwhelms. It repairs the past and provides new insight and information into why things happened the way they did, who or what is to blame (not you), and why it affected you like it did. Bringing this understanding and healing to these small areas allows you to heal and seal these deep wounds.

The 10 Benefits of Titration for Trauma Recovery

Titration can help us recover from trauma by (Hanson, 2016)

1. **Integration:** Integrating our body, mind, and emotions to successfully process and integrate trauma.
2. **Nervous system regulation:** Titration creates a space where we can settle with the past, regulate our emotions and physiological experiences, and find resolution. This allows us to reach a calmed state.
3. **Recovery of sense of self:** Through this process, we can address areas where trauma has made you feel lost, broken, or unworthy, and heal these areas.
4. **Healing Shock:** Creating a space where trauma can be revisited in a managed state decreases the

amount of shock the body experiences during traumatic flashbacks and panic attacks.
5. **Stops re-traumatization:** Decreasing the effect trauma has on us by addressing and healing it in increments, helps us stop re-traumatization.
6. **Obtain information:** Titration allows you to focus on small memories and gain better insight into them.
7. **De-repression:** Titration reverses the repression of distressing emotions and memories, allows emotions to resurface, and encourages us to address and work through them.
8. **Repairing the past:** Titration brings healing to the past through a deeper understanding of the event and ourselves.
9. **Nervous system repair and recovery:** Regulating the nervous system allows it to recover its functions and free us from a frozen state.
10. **Decoupling:** Titration helps us realize that not everything is linked or that emotions are coupled. In toxic and unhealthy environments and relationships, we may be subjected to mental, emotional, and physical abuse, narcissistic behavior, and emotional manipulation. Even though these relationships cause pain and heartbreak, we often find ourselves returning to these people or environments, seeking validation or love. Titration works to decouple the skewed perception that pain equates to love.

Balancing Emotional Responses

When we balance our emotions, we are no longer controlled by distressing or overwhelming feelings. This life skill promotes emotional resilience and mental clarity. Balancing our emotional responses reduces the effect that emotional waves or dysregulation can have on our bodies. These are some of the ways you can regulate your emotions during titration (Schmelzer, 2015):

- **Experience your emotions.** Using mindfulness, pay attention to how you feel for a few minutes. Can you label these emotions? Expand on what you are feeling.
- **Become an observer of emotions.** Watching how others express their emotions and behave improves our understanding of how people feel. Do this by people watching or enjoying a movie with emotional content.
- **Write it down.** Cultivate present-moment awareness and understanding by writing down your thoughts, sensations, and emotions throughout the day.
- **Distract yourself.** Allow your mind to be distracted and redirected when you notice some irritation, anxiety, or frustration arising. Do something productive that takes your mind off of the negatives. These activities can include a shopping trip, a scenic walk, reading a book, or a satisfying cleaning session.

- **Use short mantras.** In the same way that self-affirmations can improve your mental and emotional attitude, creating short mantras can help you push through emotional waves and bad days. Examples of these mantras can be

  - I'm going to make it through.
  - I can do this.
  - I'm doing okay.

- **Create distance between yourself and your emotions.** Learn to separate yourself from your current problem by writing it down. Place this written problem in a box or jar and come back to it once you have devised a plan to address it.

Applying Titration in Self-Recovery

Titration helps you overcome traumatic events and memories in small doses and heals your negative emotional, physical, and mental reactions. Altering these areas allows you to find your way back to a healthier version of who you were and how you lived before trauma took over. You can find yourself again and find freedom from trauma-related expressions by identifying your triggers, gradually exposing yourself to negative memories, and releasing them through journaling.

Identifying Triggers

Triggers can spark parts or whole memories of trauma which may result in expressions of panic, helplessness, and overwhelming emotions. These events can make it feel as if we are right back in a traumatic event and reliving every moment, sensation, and thought. Triggers occur when we feel unsafe or threatened. Distressing feelings we experience once triggered are our bodies' defense mechanisms against threats. Intrusive thoughts that come with the flashbacks influence how we react emotionally.

When flashbacks occur, it can feel as if it came out of nowhere, but most likely a trigger occurred. Triggers can be subtle and be found in your everyday environment. Something as common as a toddler throwing a tantrum with a high-pitched shriek can be the trigger that takes you down a nightmarish memory lane. Identifying a trigger is important to learning to manage it. When you experience flashbacks and distressing sensations, sift through your thoughts, feelings, and environments. Question what you heard, saw, felt, or smelled. When triggers are identified, you will begin to see how events, feelings, or sights are connected and how they affect our emotional or behavioral reactions.

There are two types of triggers you need to be aware of: internal and external. *Internal triggers* are feelings and experiences within us that cause flashbacks. These triggers can be feelings of anger or anxiety, loneliness, a loss of control, memories of abandonment, or feeling vulnerable. *External triggers* refer to our environments or outside factors that cause flashbacks. These triggers can be specific dates, events, an argument, witnessing an altercation, work stress, smells, and sounds, or how someone acts.

When we find our emotions and physical expressions taking a turn, we can learn to work through our triggered reactions by doing the following (Porter, 2023):

- Find a safe place. This can be a physical setting or a memory that brings positivity, comfort, and support.
- If you are experiencing a flashback, imagine that you are seeing this imagery on a TV screen. Take control by visualizing a remote appearing in your hand and changing the channel to an image you'd rather become absorbed in.
- Practice mindful breathing to bring yourself down from a heightened state.
- Do a grounding exercise that utilizes three of your senses to foster present-moment awareness and distraction from unwelcome memories and emotions.
- Pre-record self-assuring and supportive voice notes that you can play and listen to to help you out of this state.
- Distract yourself from whatever you are experiencing by calling a friend, singing a song, or caressing your pet.
- Practice self-soothing and self-care practices to induce feelings of calm and safety.

- Be mindful of what you are experiencing and think about what you can do to support yourself through this moment.
- Avoid triggers you are aware of.

Gradual Exposure

Gradual exposure is the paced revisiting of traumatic memories, distressing situations, and phobias. When we fear certain things, we tend to avoid them but this tends to make things worse. Avoidance or poor exposure builds no resilience or tolerance to these challenges. Exposure therapy helps you confront and conquer your fears and create understanding and realistic beliefs about what you are afraid of.

Gradual exposure therapy can be experienced through a host of exposure approaches. The form of exposure therapy you participate in may depend on your needs or the extent of trauma and your responses to it (Cleveland Clinic, 2023).

- **Imaginal exposure therapy** uses the vivid visualization of objects, people, places, or events we fear. This therapy involves vividly imagining the thing, situation, or activity you fear.
- **In vivo exposure therapy** asks you to face your fears in real life. This can be done through activities or image exposure.
- **Interoceptive exposure therapy** invites you to experience your body's physical responses to trauma and become less affected by it.

- **Virtual reality exposure therapy** incorporates virtual reality to simulate that which you fear.
- **Graded exposure** asks you to list what you fear according to its intensities, such as from mild to extreme.
- **Flooding** asks you to list what you fear from most extreme to mild fear.
- **Prolonged exposure therapy** is when we gradually approach memories, feelings, and thoughts related to trauma through a three-month process. This is most effective for people with post-traumatic stress disorder (PTSD).
- **Systematic desensitization** involves exposure activities and relaxation exercises to help you associate fears with positivity and calming techniques.

Exposure therapy not only decreases your response and sensitivity to what you fear or what makes you anxious, but it can improve other areas of your life as well. Exposure weakens how you may have previously associated what you fear with bad outcomes. It builds your confidence in your ability to confront and overcome fear and anxiety and learn to manage them. It allows you to become more comfortable with experiencing fear as you develop a more realistic, and less emotional perspective on fearfulness. Gradual exposure therapy improves the way we function, develops mental and emotional stability, and improves our social skills.

Journaling

Expressing yourself in writing is a way to release what you are unable to verbalize, fully confront just yet, or find support when you cannot rely on anyone else. Journaling can bring health and healing to our physical, mental, and emotional state, decrease persistent troubling thoughts, and decrease stress and symptoms of depression. Journals allow us to write expressively and be vulnerable without facing external judgment.

As we unlock trapped traumatic memories, we can express strong emotions and release them. This cultivates and nurtures our ability to be self-aware, practice introspection, validate how we feel, and regain control of our minds and emotions. Exposing our inner selves in this manner helps us to identify and analyze triggers and patterns and lets us track our personal growth. When we journal our way through this journey, we can look back at all we survived and accomplished and celebrate our progress.

Challenges Experienced on This Journey

It's not always natural or easy to journal our feelings, thoughts, and emotions. Especially, when our inner self-critic has somehow found a megaphone. Throw in addressing and releasing trauma, and you may find yourself with some new hurdles. These are the challenges you may come across as you learn to journal trauma (Van Horn, 2023):

Resistance or Fear

You may be afraid that writing down a traumatic event may trigger unwanted memories and sensations. Maybe you're not prepared to face it right now. You've had a good day and the possibility of it turning sour is too much. Well, since you're in charge, you can stop or begin writing at any point. Start slowly and come back when you're comfortable.

Emotional Overwhelm

Journaling can be emotionally taxing. Learn to pace yourself when it comes to heavy topics. When it becomes overwhelming, take a break and think of or write down positive memories or what you are grateful for. Distract yourself with activities or supportive friends to get your mind away from a distressed state.

Lack of Motivation or Consistency

Journaling does not have to be boring. Incorporate colors and stickers or change up what you will write about today. Write down any dreams, goals, and funny thoughts you have.

Coping With Potential Triggers

As you explore experiences and memories, you will begin to recognize trauma triggers. If journaling activates a trigger, create resources in your journal to help you navigate that experience.

How to Journal With Trauma

- Create a safe and comfortable space to journal. Design an atmosphere that lowers your guard and allows you to be vulnerable. Incorporate low lighting, candles, scents, plush pillows, and herbal teas. Don't forget your box of tissues!
- Simply write what comes to mind. Write continuously and use prompts when you get stuck.
- Don't judge your writing skills, penmanship, your emotions, thoughts, or how you are expressing yourself. Additionally, refrain from blaming yourself for past events as you revisit them. This is a zone free from self-criticism.
- On the days that you address and express traumatic events, reflect on who you were at that stage. Conjuring up an image of yourself at that time may help to better visualize the event and bring understanding to it and how it affected you.

Interactive Element

Identifying Triggers

In today's activity, we're going to delve into a traumatic memory and bring an understanding of the triggers. Follow these prompts to highlight possible triggers associated with an event, how this affects you, and how you still perceive this event. Begin this exercise by bringing specific events you found traumatizing to mind.

1. What are the negative thoughts and emotions you have right now?
2. What are the physical reactions you are experiencing?
3. How does this relate to your trauma?
4. How has this altered the way you react?
5. How has this event affected your relationships?

After you have completed this activity, take a moment to center yourself. Bring out your journal or answer these questions aloud. Use these prompts to gain self-understanding and foster a healthier movement forward.

- What are the current sensations you are feeling after the above activity?
- Is your response to the traumatic event extreme or have you become less sensitive to it over time?
- What can you do to balance your emotional reaction to this memory?
- How has this experience made you stronger?
- What is your favorite activity that makes you happy and calm?

Titration is a method of trauma healing that allows you to be the captain of your own vessel. Slowly visiting different areas of trauma helps us create centralized care and management in these areas. You can spend as much time addressing, healing, and developing an understanding of each small area until you are satisfied with the result. Gradual exposure therapy reduces the effect that trauma has on your mind, emotions, and body. Trigger identification guides you into self-awareness and mindful activities that decrease your sensitivity to common sounds that lead to activation. Trigger awareness helps us make decisions that no longer put us in states of stress, anxiety, or overwhelm. Creating healthy boundaries within ourselves and with others goes a long way to improving our overall well-being.

Titration lets us manage our self-care in a way that is opposite to experiencing trauma. This method stops us from experiencing re-traumatization and we heal fractured memories and hurt areas, become aware of our triggers, and learn to become less sensitive to them. Instead of living as a ball of unease, anxiety, and stress, we are now able to unwind and become flexible to our environment. (If your trigger-related traumatic experiences are extreme or debilitating, please seek professional help in the form of trauma recovery therapists).

NINE

Setting Boundaries—Developing Healthy Limits

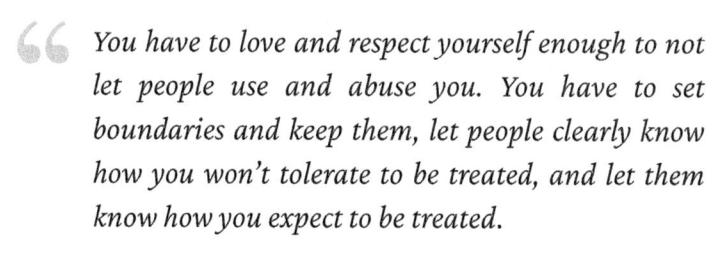

> *You have to love and respect yourself enough to not let people use and abuse you. You have to set boundaries and keep them, let people clearly know how you won't tolerate to be treated, and let them know how you expect to be treated.*
>
> Jeanette Coron

The Importance of Boundaries

Boundaries are important to how we act or feel in different environments. They require us to be self-aware and reflect on our personal desires and expectations of others and ourselves. Boundaries ensure that we receive the respect, care, love, and trust in our close circles and that we show to others. Do you receive these qualities from your relationships? Bring to mind a particular friend or event. Do you feel as if they treat you the same as other members of the group? Was your advice acknowledged or were you ignored? Does it feel as if some family members expect you to always give of yourself and time? If your answers to these questions were negative, you may have trouble with healthy boundaries.

The inability to set healthy boundaries is rooted in many things. It can be a result of growing up in a household where no one respected each other's boundaries, seeking external approval or validation, having poor self-esteem, or a fear of rejection or criticism. When we do not have healthy boundaries, we may feel as if we are bending over backward for others, always on the go, taken for granted, unloved, and exhausted. Unhealthy boundaries can foster negative emotions toward ourselves and others, affect our work environment and social relationships, and lead to poor mental and emotional health.

Setting healthy boundaries is important to cultivating a happy and fruitful life. Healthy boundaries build our self-confidence and self-respect and allow us to be our unique selves. You don't need external validation when you live according to your terms. When you have boundaries, you can express needs and desires and receive them. Healthy boundaries help us understand another's point of view and respect them, guide us to stand our ground, avoid resentment and conflict, and set consequences when others violate these boundaries (Andrade, 2021). Healthy boundaries ensure that your physical, mental, and emotional health remains a priority.

The Different Types of Boundaries

Before setting healthy boundaries, it's important to define the areas that we should have them in. Boundaries are here to protect and nurture your space. These are the five types of boundaries:

1. **Physical** boundaries protect your personal space, privacy, and your body.
2. **Sexual** boundaries verbalize your needs, expectations, or language that makes you uncomfortable.
3. **Intellectual** boundaries express your thoughts and beliefs.
4. **Emotional** boundaries let others know when you are not ready to express your feelings.
5. **Financial** boundaries define how you prefer to use your money and whether you are comfortable sharing your account details, loaning money, or sharing a joint bank account.

How to Fortify Porous Boundaries

Unhealthy boundaries tend to be porous. This happens when we have a hard time standing up for ourselves or saying "no." When you have porous boundaries, you develop a pattern of putting others' needs above your own. If you notice that you have porous boundaries, here are ways to create healthier limits with others.

- **Become mindful:** Tune into what you are feeling and thinking. Porous boundaries can have us chasing after other's desires and have us ignoring our own. Listen to your feelings and thoughts and act accordingly.
- **Work on your limitations:** Set a limit to how many things you get roped into or feel the need to say "yes" to and decrease persistent exhaustion and overwhelm.
- **Have interests and hobbies:** Shift your main focus from others onto yourself. Explore your interests and enjoy them as a self-care ritual. This way, you already have plans when others *need* something from you.
- **Assert yourself:** Being direct when establishing your boundaries fosters respect for your desires and expectations.

Why Boundaries Are Crucial for Emotional Health

When we find ourselves doing things we have no interest in, are around people we do not particularly enjoy, or feel both obligated and conditioned to do tasks, this affects how we feel. Sometimes, negative emotions creep into our minds when we are helping others. You may love these individuals, but you wish they could just help themselves. They are probably capable of doing a lot, but it's more convenient for you to do it for them.

These experiences can foster negative emotions towards them and yourself. Your inner critic may rear its head and let you know how weak you are when you cannot stand up for yourself. Harboring these emotions contributes to a troubled emotional state. When we are constantly unhappy, our emotional health suffers. Boundaries are crucial to expressing ourselves and setting limits so we do not find ourselves in positions where we are taken advantage of, disrespected, emotionally drained, exploited, or treated like a doormat.

Challenges in Setting Boundaries

Setting boundaries can be challenging when we have not done so before. Changing the way you may have previously acted can be quite a shock for those you enjoyed your weak or lack of boundaries. Before we can change and fortify porous boundaries, we need to identify what they are rooted in. If you have struggled with setting boundaries or maintaining them, it can be for these reasons (Lee, 2018).

Fear of Missing Out (FOMO)

FOMO can cause us to overcommit and overextend ourselves to others because we don't want to miss out on any excitement, fun, or engagement. This can make our lives a bit chaotic and leave little room to attend to our needs and desires.

Perfectionism

Wanting to bring your best to the table 24/7 is exhausting! Perfectionism may have you saying "yes" to too many opportunities because saying "no" makes you look weak. It can lead to people pleasing and constantly having to prove yourself. This obsessive behavior makes it difficult to just be yourself.

Social Conditioning

For some of us, our identities are tied up in what we do for others. Especially, for us women of whom much is expected and demanded. Not to mention all the titles that come with womanhood, such as sister, mother, wife, caretaker, breadwinner, and so on and all the work that comes with it. With the social norms that come with these roles, we may feel guilty about not wanting to fulfill them.

Signs of Poor Boundaries

When we are challenged in the aforementioned areas, it can be difficult to strengthen our resolve and set boundaries. These are signs that you may have a soft set of boundaries (Darvasula, 2021):

- You struggle to decide between making a decision for yourself and doing what others want you to.
- You people please by catering to other's desires or perspectives, instead of your own.
- You are overly focused on meeting other people's needs, which depletes your energy reserves and leaves you with little time to take care of yourself.
- You are giving too much to too many people, who are constantly taking from you.
- You have lost a sense of who you are in overextending your service to others.

- You tend to overshare information, thoughts, and emotions with people with whom you have not established trust or a relationship.
- You feel resentful, frustrated, or annoyed when you are coerced or conditioned into helping or joining others. Deep down you'd rather be doing something else or resting, but you couldn't say "no."
- You display passive-aggressive behavior because you are struggling to communicate your needs or wants and feelings of frustration or disappointment.
- You commit to tasks or events because of a fear of rejection or abandonment by others, such as if I don't do this for them, they won't need me anymore.

The Importance and Benefits of Setting Boundaries

Boundaries help cultivate peace and positivity in your personal and professional relationships. Healthy boundaries not only let others know how you want and deserve to be treated, but they also help you develop a clearer perspective on who does not respect them or you and can ultimately lead you to healthier friendships and relationships that nurture positivity, growth, and mutual respect. As your healthy boundaries strengthen, you will find that you're enjoying life more, you experience fewer problematic encounters, and you enjoy people and activities that align with your values and beliefs.

What Healthy Boundaries Look Like

A healthy boundary means that you can effectively communicate your thoughts and feelings. This occurs when you understand what your thoughts and feelings are telling you and learn to vocalize your limits.

Healthy boundaries mean

- being assertive and saying "no" to activities or conversations you are uncomfortable with or that go against your core beliefs and values.
- refusing blame or guilt laid at your door when it is not yours to carry, such as through emotional manipulation or projection.
- removing yourself from an environment that hurts or disrespects you.
- learning to decipher and stand up for your own feelings and perspectives in group settings or relationships.
- learning to have an independent identity within a friendship or relationship.
- identifying and vocalizing areas you need support in and where you do not.
- asking for space when you need to be alone.
- sticking up for yourself when someone says something unkind, incorrect, or unjustified.
- communicating when someone has hurt you or crossed a limit or boundary.
- sharing what you are comfortable with and being vulnerable at your own pace.

- having a right to privacy in relationships and friendships.
- changing your mind and boundaries as you mature without guilt.
- dictating your time, such as when and with whom you spend your time, or when it is a self-care day.
- setting boundaries for your own behavior and navigating unhealthy or negative emotions.
- expressing sexual desires, needs, discomforts, or limits.
- expressing your beliefs and the need for others to respect them.
- remaining true to your principles and not feeling pressured to hide or change them.
- communicating what your body needs, such as changing your diet or speaking to the doctor when you feel ill.
- deciding what material possessions you would like to share and what you would not, such as in friendships or relationships. This extends to finances as well.

Identifying Boundary Issues

To get us to the point where we can develop strong, healthy boundaries, we need to look at the areas in our lives that need our attention. We need to identify what is weakening our resolve to simply do or say what we desire. Use these four points to recognize areas where you need stronger boundaries (Tartakovsky, 2014):

1. **Tune into your emotions.** How do you feel when someone keeps asking you to do something for them? Take note of which emotions surface. Is it annoyance, fear, or frustration? Is it joy or happiness? Become attuned to how you are feeling and let this govern whether or not you need a boundary in this area. Negative emotions mean you may need to distance yourself from this individual and create a boundary.
2. **Tune into your thoughts.** Do you find that you have more self-critical thoughts or a sense of unease around some people? Perhaps, there have been one too many times that have sent snide comments your way. Acknowledge the thoughts you have around certain people and create boundaries that distance you from them.
3. **Ask others.** Ask your friends about any boundaries they may have. Use them as examples of how to set your own and achieve their level of peace. Compare boundaries within your friendship group and observe how and where they have benefitted them.
4. **Get clear on your values**: Identify what matters most to you. What do you prioritize or want to achieve? Change the way you think, act, or prioritize others over yourself to make this happen.

Self-Reflective Questions

We may not always know that we are in need of boundaries. Especially, when meek behavior is expected of us or conditional relationships weaken our self-esteem and lead to soft boundaries. In identifying where we need boundaries, we need to discern areas where we need more self-respect, power, acknowledgment, or love. Use these questions to bring awareness to your boundaries (Robboy, n.d.).

- Who has made me feel insecure, hurt, frustrated, sad, or angry after socializing with them?
- How do I typically interact with them?
- Have I done anything in the past to control the situation?
- What methods have or haven't worked?
- What behaviors or actions would I like to stop that others direct at me?
- What things do people say that undermine my self-confidence and self-esteem?
- Do people at work pressure me to engage in conversations that I feel interfere with work?
- Do my friends assume that I'm comfortable about certain topics that I'm not?
- Do I feel overwhelmed when people ask me for favors?
- What things do my friends say about others that make me uncomfortable?
- What do I feel uncomfortable sharing with others?
- Do I feel the need to change my behavior in different social group settings?
- Do I feel pressured into participating in activities that I'd rather not?
- What situations make me feel defensive?
- Who do I feel confident asserting a need with?

- Is there someone I feel would disrespect my personal space and values?
- In which areas can I learn to be more flexible?
- In which situations do I need to have my guard up?
- What past event has made interactions with certain people uncomfortable?
- What do I want to prevent from happening in the future?

Creating Healthy Boundaries

Healthy boundaries develop the foundation for you to speak your mind, become who you want to be, and improve your self-perspective. Setting boundaries defines what and where your mental, emotional, and physical limits are. Healthy boundaries foster security, nurture healthy relationships, and reduce anxiety. These are the strategies you can utilize to set and maintain your boundaries (Pattemore, 2021):

- Self-reflect and discover why setting boundaries in certain areas is important to you. Where and what are your feelings rooted in? How will setting these boundaries improve your emotional well-being?
- Create and introduce your boundaries slowly. This is a great chance for you and those in your circle. Do it at your own pace and observe if this boundary guides you in the right direction.
- Set boundaries at the beginning of your friendships and relationships to decrease negative emotions and future disappointment.

- Consistently enforce your boundaries. When we allow others to dismiss our boundaries, they are encouraged to place new expectations and demands on us. Strong and steady boundaries reinforce our initial thresholds, desires, and beliefs, and our boundary lines are respected.
- Use boundaries to design self-care and personal time every week to prioritize your well-being and happiness.
- Don't be afraid to incorporate extra boundaries in certain areas of your life. For instance, workplace boundaries can improve your performance, avoid stress, improve your relationships with your coworkers, and foster job satisfaction.
- Set social media boundaries that cultivate a positive experience and benefit your mental health. Make your profile private, share posts only with specific individuals, or mute your comment sections. These boundaries protect your peace of mind.
- Engage in self-love activities to boost your mental and emotional attitude and feed you with positivity. This can change the way you perceive your worth and motivate you to implement healthy boundaries.
- Let your gut instinct guide your boundary setting. Don't overthink what you are feeling or allow strong emotions and inflexibility to dictate your boundaries. Rigid boundaries can negatively impact your health and relationships, just as porous boundaries can.

When Boundaries Are Violated

When you first begin setting and implementing your boundaries, no matter how small they are, you are bound to step on a few toes. When you had weak boundaries, there may have been many individuals who profited off your labor and your inability to say "no." In most cases, these people knew exactly what they were doing and expected you to do their bidding. It can be hard to break out of your past mold and in these early stages, you may face some external resistance. These are the signs that your boundaries are being violated:

- You have to remind someone of your boundaries over and over again.
- You have to justify the reasons behind your boundaries.
- You have to express how uncomfortable you feel or tell others to stop their behavior when they ignore or disrespect a boundary.
- You are interrupted or dismissed when expressing an important thought or feeling.
- Your requests are mocked or they do the opposite of them.
- You experience external pressure to change or amend your boundaries (for their benefit).

If you experience negative emotions toward something, someone, or an event, your boundaries have likely been violated.

What to Do When Boundaries Are Being Violated

When you find yourself feeling overwhelmed, anxious, distressed, or angry when you have tried to stand up for yourself, here's what you need to do:

- Consistently set and reiterate your boundaries until you receive the results you want.
- Record when and how your boundaries were violated and your response to them. Reflect on these events and analyze where you can strengthen your boundaries.
- Don't allow your boundaries to be pushed back on. Assert what you will and will not accept and stand by it.
- Adapt your response to boundary violations. It helps not to feed into narcissistic individuals, who often use violations to get a rise out of you.
- You are in control of who gets to share your space. Limit or eliminate your interactions with people who make you uneasy or disrespect your boundaries.

Interactive Element

Understanding Your Boundaries

To help define and bring awareness to how to set your boundaries, maintain them, or why you need them, reflect on the ten prompts below:

1. What are my core values? How do they align with my boundaries?
2. Which areas do I struggle to set boundaries in? Why is this a challenge for me?
3. What are my ideal boundaries in a relationship?
4. Do I feel guilty when asserting my boundaries?
5. How has other's treatment of me affected my self-esteem and self-worth?
6. What boundaries can I put in place to heal and improve these areas?
7. In what ways have porous boundaries sabotaged me?
8. What is a boundary I wish I made years ago?
9. How has setting boundaries improved my relationship with myself?
10. Reflect on a time when doing something for someone evoked negative emotions. What kind of boundary can change that experience?

Setting boundaries can be your lifelong best friend. Instead of finding yourself in an exhausting, self-sabotaging, and unsatisfying way of living, creating healthy boundaries liberates us from conditioned and coerced behavior. It gives you a platform to voice your wants and needs and helps you develop the confidence to stand up for yourself. Maintaining healthy boundaries ensures that you finally receive the same care, love, and effort that you've given, and when you don't, you now have the courage to walk away from what no longer benefits you or nurtures your growth. Set healthy, flexible boundaries that allow you to prioritize your emotional well-being, develop healthy friendships and relationships, build your self-esteem to go after what you want, and cultivate life satisfaction. Healthy boundaries and healing practices motivate you to live life on your terms, incorporate mindfulness, cultivate positivity, and bring hope back to your life.

TEN

Integrative Recovery—Combining Somatic Therapy With Other Approaches

> *As you heal, you see yourself more realistically. You accept that you are a person with strengths and weaknesses. You make the changes you can in your life and let go of the things that aren't in your power to change. You learn that every part of you is valuable. And you realize that all of your thoughts and feelings are important, even when they're painful or difficult.*
>
> Ellen Bass

The Holistic Approach

Holistic health is centered around healing that makes us feel whole. It focuses on addressing and catering to the needs of your body, mind, spirit, and social relationships. The holistic approach teaches that these areas of the body are connected and influenced by one another. To truly heal ourselves, we have to pay attention to all these areas. Combining the practices encouraged in this book and additional somatic therapies effectively releases traumatic memories imprinted on our minds and bodies and motivates us to start living. The holistic approach guides us to creating routines and life-long tools that prioritize our mental, emotional, and physical health, and promote wellness.

Principles of Holistic Healing Therapy

Holistic healing therapy has a set of principles that enable balance and harmony within our mind, body, and spirit. These principles acknowledge the true meaning of healing, what it takes to get there, and why it is so important for our health. These are the six principles of holistic healing therapy that work to heal deep wounds and change the way we have been living (*What Is the Importance of Holistic Healing Therapy?*, 2021):

1. **Healing the whole person:** We are more than just physical beings. Holistic healing observes all facets of who we are and works to bring healing to these areas.
2. **Unique individual, unique care:** We are all unique and our lifestyles differ from each other. Holistic healing provides various techniques and personalized care that can be tailored to your work schedule, environment, flexibility, comfortability, or level of trauma.

3. **Targeting the root cause:** Holistic healing identifies and treats the root causes of areas of concern, challenges, and trauma. As we discover the root cause, we can make the changes that will improve and heal these areas.
4. **Natural healing techniques:** Holistic healing makes use of natural and noninvasive methods such as herbal teas, dietary changes, mindful eating, and massages that develop a positive and relaxing state of being.
5. **Creating balance and harmony:** In holistic healing, we learn to create a balance between our personal, private, and professional lives, learn to manage stress, and cultivate contentment and inner satisfaction.
6. **Cultivation of spiritual fulfillment:** Here, we are encouraged to find purpose and meaning in life by exploring our spiritual needs and connecting with ourselves.

The Trauma-Informed Care Approach

Holistic healing therapy follows a trauma-informed care approach, which recognizes how trauma impacts our mental, emotional, behavioral, and physical health. Trauma can alter how our body functions physically, emotionally, and neurologically. This is a comprehensive approach that brings understanding to past traumatic events we have experienced and combines it into our individual treatments. Trauma-informed care recognizes the impact of trauma on our mental and emotional health. Among its treatment plans, this approach incorporates cognitive behavioral therapy that guides us to break free of self-destructive cycles.

Trauma-informed care fosters lasting positive change by

- bringing awareness to the many facets and effects of trauma.
- creating a safe environment for ourselves.
- allowing us to navigate our own healing process through individualized care.
- building self-understanding and validating our emotions.
- empowering us with the tools to regain control of our lives.
- motivating us to share our experiences, struggles, or challenges, and foster healing through a support system.

Health Benefits of Holistic Healing Therapy

Holistic healing practices work to release stored negative energy, making more room for positivity, joy, and growth in your life. Healing therapy provides physical, psychological, emotional, and spiritual benefits.

Physical Benefits

- reduces and helps manage chronic pain
- improves digestion and gut health
- increases physical flexibility
- decreases chronic fatigue

- improves our sleep quality
- boosts our immune function

Psychological Benefits

- reduces stress and anxiety
- helps balance emotions
- improves cognitive function
- builds resilience against addiction

Emotional Benefits

- enhances our quality of life
- encourages us to prioritize ourselves through self-care
- helps us to make informed decisions for our health
- releases stored trauma and emotions associated with it

Spiritual Benefits

- guides us to spiritual fulfillment
- further develops our mindfulness

Why the Holistic Approach Is Important

Talk therapies do well to address stored trauma, but in order to heal and move on from a stuck position, we need to go the extra mile. This is where holistic healing comes in. Trauma therapy works on the mind, but when we combine it with somatic therapy, we encompass the whole body and provide healing to it.

As we focus on physical and emotional self-awareness and incorporate movement, breathwork, and mindfulness, we can reconnect with our bodies and process trauma to permanently release both it and the hold it has had on our lives. The holistic approach is pivotal to healing and mending deep wounds so that they no longer stop us from living.

Complementary Therapies

The best thing about integrative therapy is that you can combine a variety of therapies and practices that align with your interests, values, and lifestyle. Therapies such as talk therapy, eye movement desensitization and reprocessing (EMDR), and creative therapy can be combined with somatic practices to enhance your healing journey and elevate your quality of life.

Talk Therapy

Talk therapies help us vocalize troubling thoughts, emotions, expressions, and behaviors. It is a safe space where we can freely express ourselves, pinpoint where trauma is rooted, and develop solutions to overcome hurdles in life (Lindberg, 2023). Talk therapy helps us to

- identify the root causes of distress.
- navigate through self-sabotaging behaviors.
- understand thoughts and feelings caused by stressful events in our lives.
- understand our emotions and behavior.

- identify obstacles to achieving mental health.
- overcome insecurities.
- reduce and manage stress and anxiety.
- address traumatic experiences, memories, and triggers.
- break unhealthy habits.
- change and improve our lifestyles.

Types of Talk Therapy

Talk therapy is divided into five different approaches. Each of these approaches is designed to address specific areas you find challenging. These five talk therapy types can be combined with each other and somatic therapy for your ideal healing journey.

1. **Behavioral therapy:** This therapy helps us to address and let go of unhealthy behavior and adopt healthier practices.
2. **CBT:** Cognitive behavioral therapy helps us to recognize self-sabotaging thoughts and behaviors and change them.
3. **Humanistic therapy:** This therapy helps us develop a healthy and positive sense of self. In humanistic therapy, you explore your strengths and feelings, discover more about yourself, and find purpose and meaning in your life.
4. **Psychodynamic therapy:** This therapy brings understanding to the motivation behind how we feel, think, and act.

5. **Holistic or integrative therapy:** This approach combines different therapies, theories, and practices to design the ideal healing therapy to meet your specific needs.

EMDR

Eye movement desensitization and reprocessing therapy involves moving your eyes in a specific way as you follow the movements of a designated object while remembering traumatic events. This form of talk therapy helps the brain process trauma-related memories, such as distressing flashbacks, emotions, and the physical manifestations of stored trauma, and reduces the impact they have on our minds, emotions, bodies, and spirits. Unlike the aforementioned types of talk therapy, EMDR does not require you to give detailed information about a traumatic event. It aims to change trauma-associated emotions, thoughts, and feelings. This approach focuses on healing the brain. EMDR relies on how the brain processes and stores memories.

Adaptive information processing (AIP) states that if our information processing system is impaired, our memories are stored in a raw, unprocessed, and maladaptive form. Your brain stores normal and unpleasant memories in different ways. During normal positive memories, smooth, fast networking between your brain cells occurs, which is why our senses enable us to re-experience memories. When we experience a distressing event, our brain goes offline and how it networks is changed. This results in a disconnect between what we are experiencing through our senses and what our brain stores as memories of the event.

The way our brain stores trauma after highly distressing events can make it difficult to heal fully, as our brain still believes there is a threat in our environment. When our senses are triggered, these unprocessed emotions can induce overwhelming fear, anxiety, and panic—taking us right back into the danger zone. EMDR helps us access these stored memories through combined eye movement and guided instructions to access them. This helps us reprocess what we remember, repair the negative effects it has had on our mental health, and better manage trauma-associated feelings.

The Phases of EMDR

EMDR therapy is a way to help people deal with trauma by following a simple, step-by-step process. The initial phase of this process begins by talking about challenges you are having difficulty overcoming and creating a treatment approach. This guides us through overcoming them by addressing past bad memories and what triggers our stress, to improve our mental, emotional, and physical states. As we progress through the stages, we learn how to manage trauma responses through eye movements and resourcing.

Taking a closer look at traumatic memories allows us to understand how they affect our thoughts, emotions, and behavior, and we can rate just how great we experience them. Through EMDR practices, we can constantly evaluate how the effects of trauma on our minds and bodies are reducing. Utilizing this therapy desensitizes us to past traumas so that they become less distressing. While these areas improve, we are able to incorporate positivity to build mental and emotional resilience where trauma once wreaked havoc.

Throughout the EMDR process, you are constantly evaluating negative memories and traumatic expressions and processing them until the negativity is alleviated. Positive memories are adopted and instilled so that there is no space for traumatic memories to resurge or new experiences to send us spiraling. Finally, we revisit our progress to ensure there are no setbacks, using any new insights to help even more in future sessions, effectively starting the process over if necessary. This approach allows for gradual healing, ensuring each step builds on the last toward overcoming trauma.

Eye movement desensitization and reprocessing therapy is a process with eight phases. Each of these phases is the step taken in therapy to identify, acknowledge, and vocalize traumatic experiences and emotional expression in a less distressing manner until we can manage the effects of trauma (Corcoran, 2024).

Phase One: History-Taking and Treatment Planning

The first part of EMDR involves assessing the area you are struggling with or feeling stuck in by targeting past memories and triggers and exploring how you can overcome this and reach your goals.

Phase Two: Preparation

As we develop a treatment plan, we are exposed to eye-movement practices and calm place exercises to develop resources for our trauma-healing journey.

Phase Three: Assessment

This phase requires us to revisit traumatic memories and assess how they affect our thought processes and body sensations. These areas are assessed to evaluate our changes in emotions and thought processing through the validity of cognition (VOC) scale and subjective units of disturbance (SUD) scale.

VOC measures how true or false a question related to the past is on a scale of one to seven, where one is completely false and seven is true.

SUD measures the scale of disturbance after an emotion is named. The disturbance rates are on a scale of zero to ten, where zero rates as no disturbance and ten rates as an extreme level of disturbance.

Phase Four: Desensitization

Desensitization is achieved as we observe our memories and incorporate eye movements and bilateral stimulations (BLS), such as tapping to revisit trauma areas until they become less distressing.

Phase Five: Installation

The goal here is to start believing in ourselves and building resilience. Phase five occurs after a memory is no longer distressing and positive beliefs are reinforced.

Phase Six: Body Scan

Body scanning enables us to observe how our bodies react to a past traumatic memory with the help of positive installation. If you are still experiencing negative effects, reprocessing continues utilizing BLS methods.

Phase Seven: Closure

When the memory you were working on is fully processed, we adopt techniques and practices that keep us in a healthy and positive space until the next EMDR session.

Phase Eight: Re-Evaluation

After you have found closure in one area, we revisit it to ensure that there are no relapses, that the techniques have been effective, and to uncover new insight into the memories and ourselves. These memories and new information become the focus of your following EMDR session, starting with phase one.

Benefits of EMDR

- It does not require detailed explanations of talk therapy which can be re-traumatizing.
- Promotes intellectual understanding of trauma and its effects by incorporating your mind, body, and emotions.

- Revisiting traumatic experiences in EMDR is a short process.
- As we recall trauma, we are also processing it.

Creativity

Creative therapy utilizes the arts to express, release, and heal the effects trauma has had on our minds, emotions, and bodies. This therapy is an effective technique that improves emotional and health conditions by enhancing the way we live life and developing a passion for the arts. Creative therapy helps us channel our thoughts and emotions through artistic expression, especially, when we struggle to express ourselves verbally. With this therapy, we can

- communicate what we cannot put into words.
- create a safe place to express ourselves without judgment.
- mature our thought processes and develop problem-solving skills.
- talk about complicated and uncomfortable feelings and difficult emotions.
- improve our social connections as we participate in creative activities.

The five artistic expressions incorporated in creative therapy include

1. **Music therapy** where listening to sounds and music can help you unlock suppressed emotions or create a positive attitude.

2. **Dance therapy** and fluid movement can help you express your thoughts and feelings, relieve muscle tension, and improve flexibility. Remember, how you physically feel can affect your emotions and mind.
3. **Poetry therapy** puts our complicated thoughts and emotions to paper. For some of us, writing will truly capture our deepest thoughts and feelings as we take time to self-reflect.
4. **Art therapy** utilizes drawing or painting to express what we see in our memories and how that makes us feel. Colors and motions have an apt way of describing and enhancing how our emotions feel.
5. **Drama therapy** incorporates re-enactment to address uncomfortable feelings and events, work through challenging experiences, and process parts of our past. It can improve our self-esteem and confidence as part of recovery therapy.

Benefits of Creative Therapy

Participating in the five types of creative therapy brings healing to our mental, emotional, and physical health, and enhances our quality of life by (Smith Haghighi, 2021)

- improving cognition
- improving sensorimotor functions
- improving self-esteem and self-awareness
- elevating social skills
- building emotional resilience
- encouraging insight into negative situations

- resolving conflict and distress
- improving our ability to build and maintain relationships
- developing greater self-understanding
- distracting us from pain and discomfort
- developing a sense of accomplishment and empowerment
- providing relaxation

Confessions: Memories, Trauma, and EMDR

I've always hated it when people say to me, "You're such a strong person" and that the things I've faced in my life have made me stronger. What's the alternative? Curl up in a ball and die? That is not an alternative! So, no, I have always gotten up, dusted myself off, and carried on as usual, but it all piles up. Negative experiences are locked away in the bank of our mind and our body, and eventually, enough is enough, you have to put a stop to it all. You've become so broken that living has lost meaning, there's nothing left of you, you don't even know who you are or how you got to this point.

Every day, you go about your business and try to do what you tell yourself you're 'supposed' to do, and you beat yourself up when you don't do it, can't be bothered to do it, or don't have the energy to do it. But let's face it, you set the most unrealistic expectations for yourself that you would never hold anyone else to.

Even though life feels hopeless, you'll find yourself smiling but there's nothing behind that smile; you hide how you feel. No one understands and some simply think we're being irrational and you're petrified that people with think you're crazy if they find out what you're thinking and feeling.

Never-ending thoughts race through your head with all the should haves or things you didn't do, and you beat yourself up for it. From the minute you wake up, these thoughts run rampant, plaguing you with conversations that will not happen and you pass judgement, or make decisions based on those conversations. These thought patterns are so damaging, especially, when these perceptions cause us to become suspicious of others, overly sensitive to external social opinions, and decrease our self-esteem. Relationships are affected because somehow you believe you know what the people around you think, feel, and know.

When someone would notice something amiss with my demeanor, they would ask me if I was okay, and I'd reply with the safe and usual "Oh, I'm just tired" or "I haven't slept well the past couple of days" or "I had a bad day at work." These responses usually do the trick, don't they? But the longer this went on, the worse my mental and emotional health became. I had terrible, horrible, angry outbursts over nothing, and it felt as if they came out of nowhere. These expressions frightened me because I had no control over them, and it escalated to the point where I expressed myself physically in a negative way. The anger eventually gave way to a deep depression and a crippling anxiety moved in. I was petrified of doing the things that I used to love doing, it robbed me of the life I loved. I was drinking more to dull the feelings, but that led to its own set of issues. I lived with the constant feeling that something awful or disastrous would happen and I overreacted to everything, every little noise.

At my lowest point, I felt nothing—no joy, anger, anxiety, love, or hunger. Only complete apathy. It felt like there was no point to anything, I couldn't care less if I ate, bathed or even moved off the couch and I became suicidal. Not because I thought the world was better off without me, but because I felt that I no longer had anything left to feel and give. The only thing that stopped me was the thought of what it would do to my loved ones. I know firsthand what it does and it almost destroyed me. I didn't want to live feeling so devoid of anything. I was numb, and it was time to get help.

My Experience With EMDR

Someone explained EMDR to me like this: A memory is like an unmarked path. You can walk down this path, but you won't know where it will take you. Bring to mind an image of your wrist and your hand. Imagine your wrist and start walking up into your hand. At your palm, your fingers represent five more paths to choose from, and each one of those is another memory linked to the one you started with.

When I started EMDR, trauma was explained to me, by way of this scenario. Imagine you were involved in a horrific car accident, you almost died, and were in the hospital for months. You had terrible injuries and had to learn to walk again. Now imagine it's two years later and you have physically recovered, you are back to work, and you are sitting in your office on the third floor of an office building. You are seated in your office chair and you are safe. Then suddenly, you hear the screeching of car brakes and a terrible crashing sound. Your body immediately tenses, your muscles tighten, your heart starts to race, and you become anxious. When you suffer severe trauma, that memory creates an abnormal pathway in your brain, kind of like a short circuit. Every time a trigger occurs, it causes the electrical impulse to go down that short circuit instead of the normal pathway, and so you react the way you would as if you were in danger. The goal of EMDR is to reroute those impulses back down through the normal pathways so that the fight or flight response of cortisol and adrenaline is not triggered.

I was instructed to find a happy memory. This was for our practice session so that I could learn the concept. I would then run this memory in my head like a movie and concentrate on it while my therapist moved her index and middle fingers back and forth a few inches in front of my face. I had to play the movie while concentrating my eyes on her fingers. Before we started, we checked in with how I was feeling; were there any parts where I felt discomfort, tight muscles, was I anxious, did I have pain anywhere, we rated everything from one to ten.

When we began, I ran the movie of a childhood memory which was picking bluebells in the woods with my mum, dad, and sister. I started to follow the fingers going back and forth, left to right in front of my eyes. The next thing I knew, I was a blubbering mess. It came out of nowhere. This was my happy memory, but why was I crying? That's when the unmarked path reference came, and she explained that even though that particular memory might have been good, it was obviously linked to other less pleasant memories, even if I didn't realize it or could recall them. We didn't continue with our practice session that day. I was instructed to think of another memory for our next session, and we would try again.

I have no explanation, but the same thing happened. Although, for some reason, what that memory was I don't recall anymore. So, we came up with plan C. It was clear to my therapist that things went a lot deeper than the one reason why we were doing EMDR in the first place, so she recommended that I come up with something imaginary. It could be a person, a place, or whatever I wanted, but it would not be related to anything in my past. I don't know where it came from, but it ended up being a place, and the more I went there, which was almost daily, the more detailed it got, the bigger the picture, so to speak. With that in place and well-practiced, we finally started EMDR!

At the beginning and end of each session, we would rate my level of anxiety and discomfort and note where that discomfort was. Slowly but surely, the numbers came down until I was no longer having severe reactions to the things that had been triggering me.

So, why did I tell you about all of this? Well, I don't want you to be afraid to try. No, it's not an easy journey, but being brave and sticking with it is utterly worth it. Trust yourself, don't give up, and take one step, one day at a time.

—Clara

Interactive Element

Prompts to Bring Self-Awareness and Direction

As you combine your knowledge and practice of holistic healing, take some time to self-reflect on your goals, desires, and changes that need to be made by answering these prompts:

- What am I passionate about?
- How much of my time is taken away by negative thoughts and emotions?
- What activities can I do to reduce negative rumination?
- What is it that I want to achieve right now?
- Where do I see myself in six months?
- What can I do to achieve this goal?
- When have I last stepped out of my comfort zone?
- Is it better for me to fail at something or never try it?
- What is a quote that really speaks to me?
- Do I treat myself with the same care and kindness as a friend I have recently supported and comforted?

The holistic healing approach is a deep penetrating therapy that combines somatic therapy with alternative complementary therapies to lead you to your best self. Incorporating deep breathing techniques, cultivating and enhancing the relationship between your mind and your body, learning mindfulness, becoming sensitive to nature's healing properties, pendulating to find healing, titrating to find balance, developing internal and external resources that combat overwhelming emotions and sensations, and reinforcing healthy habits and boundaries are revolutionary tools that not only address, heal, and release trauma but set you on a course for freedom and renewal.

When we incorporate these somatic therapies with talk therapy, EMDR, and creative therapy, we cultivate life-long change. Holistic healing therapy focuses on healing us on a mental, emotional, physical, and spiritual level, which enables us to seal up the past and leave it behind.

Thank you for taking this powerful step and choosing your healing and happiness. It's time to start giving yourself the same love and attention that you give to those around you. Choose the holistic approach and place yourself on a trajectory for emotional freedom!

Spreading the Power of Somatic Therapy

Not only can you rewrite your own story, but you also have a chance to help someone else do the same thing.

Simply by sharing your honest opinion of this book and a little about your own journey with somatic therapy, you'll inspire other people to heal their hurts and take charge of the future ahead of them.

WANT TO HELP OTHERS?

Thank you so much for your support. You're making a huge difference.

Conclusion

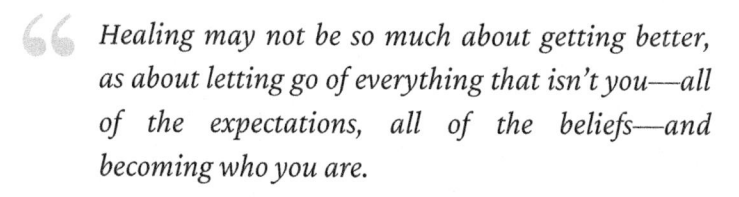

> *Healing may not be so much about getting better, as about letting go of everything that isn't you—all of the expectations, all of the beliefs—and becoming who you are.*
>
> Rachel Naomi Remen

Utilizing the Power of Somatic Therapy: The Trauma Paradox

Trauma may have us dealing with the filth and hurt someone else dumped at our front doorstep and yet we have spent so much time bearing this load as our own. Facing back-to-back trauma can chip away at our mental and emotional health, slowly diminishing the way we see, love, and trust ourselves. Experiencing and suppressing trauma can eventually alter the way we perceive life and negatively discolor it.

Many of us have faced trauma at a young and impressionable age, and that may have influenced the way we think and act for most of our lives. Some days, it can be a mission to get out of bed, leave the house, or put a smile on your face. Your mind may be filled with countless what ifs, aggrievances, and emotional overwhelm relating to what you've been dealing with for far too long. Trauma-associated behavior is often a protective mechanism and may be realized as a defensive stance that hinders us from creating friendships, an unwillingness to venture outside of our comfort zones, panic attacks or a frozen state when feeling threatened, and emotional vulnerability due to trauma suppression.

The effects of trauma can last for years, can affect all areas of our lives, and show up at the most unexpected times. When traumatic events are triggered, they can have the most unnerving physical manifestations, that can leave us feeling worse off than before. The only way we can take back control of our mind, emotions, and body is through acknowledging, addressing, and mending the root issues of our traumatic past. Somatic therapy is an approach that allows us to do this in a safe, comfortable, and soothing way, that incorporates and encourages methods intrinsic to who you are. Somatic therapy allows you to be the captain of your own ship and helps you choose your own crew members and navigate new waters with skill!

Somatic therapy works to regulate our nervous system after traumatic experiences have overstimulated and dysregulated our sympathetic nervous system. Therapeutic practices such as breathwork, mind-body awareness, grounding, pendulation, resourcing, titration, and establishing healthy boundaries are essential life skills to change your quality of life for the better by bringing ease and relaxation to it. This allows us to nurture self-respect and garner respect from others. These somatic therapy practices will guide you to achieving peace, joy, confidence, and a deep-seated satisfaction with who you are and the life you've created.

Can you remember a time before trauma changed you? How did that version of you perceive life? Did you see beauty in your environment? Did you find joy in your relationships? Does it feel as if you could have conquered the world? Somatic therapy helps to rebuild the connection we once had with ourselves, instill self-compassion and kindness to nurture self-esteem, discover feelings of inner safety, and develop resilience against negativity in our environment. Unprocessed trauma and how it has manifested no longer has to control your mind, emotions, and body. Experience the power of somatic therapy and release yourself from burdens that have kept you underfoot.

Becoming Your Own Champion

Choosing to delve deeper into somatic therapy is the first step to improving your life and taking back control. After all you've been through, it really is the time to prioritize your needs. Free yourself from if anyone once said you were weak, unlovable, or not worth it, blamed you for things that were not your fault, or invalidated your feelings, and perceptions. These were untruths used to manipulate and take advantage of you. Throughout this journey, you will have learned that you're made of much stronger stuff than what you thought. You have the ability to change where you're going. It's time to rewrite your story.

Use somatic therapy approaches to heal festering wounds and brokenness so that you can feel whole again. Become aware of the positivity in your environment and connect with those around you. Learn to listen to your body and provide it with what it needs. Bring healing to your mind, body, and soul. Take part in activities that improve your emotional and physical health. Let somatic therapy reignite your passion for life. Don't be afraid to let go of who you've become, reconnect with who you were, and create who you want to be. Recovering from trauma is not easy, but it is possible, and with the tools and insights provided in this book, you can start your journey toward emotional freedom today. Take one step at a time, pace yourself, and remember to be kind to yourself. Immerse yourself in these therapeutic practices, receive the full benefits, and let us know how well you're doing!

Bonus Chapter: Activity Workbook

This chapter contains activities for each of the somatic therapy approaches. Use these activities as additional practices to enhance your healing journey, create your own peace of mind, and release frustrations. Shake things up, try these different activities, and find what works for you!

Self-Care Practices

When it feels as if we are on the cusp of losing ourselves to external and internal static, it's important to reconnect and center ourselves. Incorporate these nine self-care activities below to prioritize and improve your overall health.

Take a Pause

Grant yourself the luxury of stillness amid the hustle. A minute of deep breathing or a moment to bask in the stillness can be a gentle reprieve in your bustling day.

Connect Wholeheartedly

Carve out a sliver of your day for heartwarming chats with those you cherish. Whether it's a swift call amid daily tasks, a cozy video catch-up, or a heartfelt conversation, these moments are the cornerstones of emotional nourishment.

Move Joyfully

Infuse your day with joyous spurts of movement. Whether it's dancing in your living room for a few minutes, a cheerful stride in the open air at noon, or playful stretches during a break, embrace these as snippets of vigor.

Breathe in the Earth

Intentionally weave in escapes to nature. Let it be as simple as a gulp of fresh air by your window, a lunch amidst greenery, or a leisurely amble through areas kissed by Mother Nature.

Choose Mindfully

Handpick the content that feeds your soul. Limit your screen indulgence, tailor your digital sphere to be a source of positivity, and reserve moments for reading that elevates or enlightens you.

Nurture Yourself

Lovingly craft rituals that coddle your spirit. It might be a tender skincare routine, savoring a tea that sings to you, or sinking into a warm bath under the cloak of dusk.

Unleash Your Inner Artist

Let the creativity flow in spontaneous bursts. Sketch, scribble, compose—any form of art that stirs delight and lets your spirit soar.

Engage Your Curiosity

Pledge a handful of minutes to hobbies that spark joy. Whether it's creating melodies, tending to a garden, or conjuring up flavors in the kitchen, these pursuits enrich your life's tapestry.

Reflect Thoughtfully

Steal moments to write down your journey. It might be morning musings or nightly thanksgivings, but let this be a sacred practice to foster self-awareness and gratitude.

Gratitude Journaling

- What are three things I experienced today that delighted me?
- What have I recently introduced into my life that's brought me peace, joy, or comfort?
- What are five things around me right now that I'm glad I don't have to live without?
- What about my environment brings me happiness?
- What are three things that make me feel like me?
- Who is someone I am thankful for and why?
- What is something I am looking forward to?
- What is the best thing that happened to me yesterday?
- Who was the last person to make me smile?
- What is my favorite thing about my partner?
- When was the last time I felt truly at peace?
- What's something my past self did that I'm grateful for today?
- What's one thing I'd like to be proud of by the end of this week/month/year?
- What do I have today that makes me happy that I didn't have a year ago?
- What makes me smile?
- What do I love most about my morning routine?
- What are things I use every day that would make my life harder if they didn't exist? (For example, your phone, a shower, a road you use, etc.)
- What is a challenge I overcame to get me to where I am today?

- What are 10 features, attributes, or accomplishments I like about myself or am proud of?
- What's something I want more of? Write a thank-you note from the perspective that you already have it.
- Who can I write a thank you letter to that I've always wanted to thank?
- What do I love about where I live?
- What is a talent or skill I'm grateful to possess?
- Who has supported me during difficult times? What would I say to them now if they were with me?
- What am I most grateful for right now?
- What emotions do I feel when I experience gratitude?

Positive Affirmations

- Just breathe!
- I am safe.
- It's okay to struggle.
- It won't always be this way.
- It's okay if all I did today was breathe.
- It's okay to feel. It's ok to feel bad.
- It's okay to let it out and express myself.
- It's okay to cry.
- It's okay to be hurting.
- It's okay to be angry.
- This, too, shall pass.

- It's okay to ask for help.
- It's okay to have a bad day, week, or month. I am still moving forward.
- It's not my fault; I am not responsible for what happened.
- My feelings are my feelings; I don't have to justify them.
- I am not a bad person.
- It's okay if I don't know what I need yet.
- I am worthy.
- I am enough.
- I am not alone.
- I do not have to be perfect.
- It's okay to prioritize myself.
- I deserve to be loved.
- I will be patient and love myself as I heal.
- Even though it might not feel like it now, everything is going to be okay!

Yoga Poses and Stretches

Whenever you feel the need to unwind, doing a few stretches can help you release tension stored in the body. These therapeutic practices foster peace of mind and flexibility and allow us to feel physically, emotionally, and mentally lighter. Follow these stretches below and enhance the way you move throughout your day!

Arm Circles

This exercise highlights your shoulder muscles and works to strengthen your biceps and triceps as you move your arms in circular motions. When doing arm circles, you can choose to either do small or large circles. Complete this exercise in whichever way feels most comfortable to you. To receive the full benefits of arm circles, make sure that you keep the tension down in your arm as you move.

This is how to perform arm circles:

1. Stand upright and engage your core.
2. Spread your arms out to the side, align them with your shoulders, and contract the muscles along your arms.
3. Begin to make slow circles with your arm as you rotate them around your shoulders. Keep your arms and elbows straight.
4. Repeat this motion for 10 counts.
5. Now, raise your arms so that they align just above your ears, and begin to rotate your arms.
6. Repeat this motion for the same amount of time.
7. Raise your arms above your head and lock your elbows.
8. Keep them raised for 10 counts.
9. Once you have completed this first set, bring your arms down, and release tension in your muscles.
10. Rest for 10 counts.
11. Complete one to two more sets if you have not yet reached your ideal state.

Cat-Cow (Standing)

The standing cat-cow pose is a favorite for those who sit in an office chair all day. It provides a deep stretch and relief for stiff muscles.

Follow these instructions to complete the cat-cow pose (Zuda Yoga, 2023):

Begin this exercise by forming the cow position.

1. Stand upright.
2. Place your hands on your hips and your draw elbows to the back.
3. Ensure that your feet are spread apart and aligned with your hips.
4. As you situate your feet, take a deep breath in and expand your chest, while titling your backside outward.

Now, let's move on to the cat position.

1. Release your breath and pull your belly inward.
2. As you exhale, bend your knees and place your hand on them.
3. Round your back and bend forward as if you are cradling an inflatable yoga ball.
4. Draw your chin down to your chest or as far as you can go.
5. Practice this stretch for three sets and make sure that you are taking full breaths throughout each step!

Standing Backbends

This exercise stretches and opens your abdominal cavity and builds strength in your back as you curve your spine backward. Begin this exercise by positioning yourself in mountain pose.

To create this pose (Pizer, 2018):

1. Stand upright with your feet together and your toes spread wide.
2. Ensure that your weight is equally distributed on your feet.
3. Keep your legs straight but not locking your knees.
4. Contract your quadriceps (large muscle at the front of your thigh) so that your knees are drawn upward.
5. Turn your thighs slightly inward.
6. Make sure you are neither tilting your pelvis forward nor tucking it inward. It should be aligned neutrally.
7. Tighten your core so that your navel is drawn inward.
8. Roll your shoulders forward and raise them toward your ears.
9. Roll them backward and bring them back down.
10. Rest your arms to the side and open your hands so that your palms are either facing the front or the side of your thighs.

Once you have taken on mountain pose, you can begin your standing backbends!

1. Take a deep breath as you raise your arms above your head.
2. Place your palms together.
3. As you exhale, gently arch your pelvis to the front and arch your back to where you feel comfortable.
4. Inhale and stand upright again.
5. Repeat this set of motions five times.

Standing Forward Fold

This exercise brings calm and relaxation as it boosts our body awareness and improves our balance. Incorporating this exercise can help manage stress and bring harmony to a dysregulated stress response by activating the parasympathetic nervous system (PNS). Bring ease to your body as you stretch tension located at the back of your body.

Engage these areas as you (Hodgson, 2022)

1. Take on mountain pose.
2. Place your hands at the side of your hips.
3. Slightly bend your knees and tilt your hips so that your abdomen folds over your legs.
4. Bend forward so that you touch your hands to the ground or your feet.
5. Take a deep breath in and lengthen your spine.
6. Exhale and straighten your legs and push your upper inner thighs to the back.

7. As you exhale, extend your torso and neck so that the top of your head is near the ground.
8. As you do the aforementioned motion, roll your shoulders back and toward your hips.

Note for Beginners

If you find that you are having difficulty reaching your toes or the ground due to poor mobility or flexibility, utilize a stepping stool, pillow, or stacked blocks, which you can stretch toward and lay your hands on. If bending over becomes painful as a result of hamstrings that are tight, bend your knees as much as you like to complete the exercise. And don't forget to create a strong and stable stance by using a thick mat and pressing your feet down, so that you can bend forward without flailing!

Standing Side Bends

This stretch helps to loosen tightness and get rid of kinks and stitches we have in our sides. As you engage in this exercise, you will feel stretches in your lower back, hips, and the sides of your abdomen.

Begin this exercise by

1. Standing upright and spreading your feet apart.
2. Place your hands at your sides and face your open palms toward your thighs.
3. Bend to your left side and slide your left arm down along your leg. Your right arm will be moving upward toward your abdomen.

4. Hold this pose for 10 counts and practice deep breathing.
5. Slowly bring yourself back up to the first position.
6. Now, bend toward your right side. Slide your right arm down your leg and feel the left one moving upward.
7. Hold this position for the same amount of time and practice deep breathing.
8. Repeat this stretch ten times.

Alternative Method

Do this exercise alongside a wall and use it for balance. Place your left palm against the wall and use it to shift outward (toward your right). Stretch your right side and hold this position for 10 counts. Once you have done this, revert to an upright position. When it's time to stretch your left side, rotate and place your right palm against the wall, and repeat the same motion.

You can also practice side bend stretches while sitting on a chair, such as seated side bends and stretching sideways so that your fingertips reach the ground.

Chest Opener

Chest opening exercises stretch our upper abdomen and train our auxiliary breathing muscles to achieve normal breathing patterns as we release tension. Abnormal or labored breathing patterns are linked to pain and stress. This exercise helps us take in more oxygen, energizes our body, stimulates cell metabolism, and improves our ability to concentrate (Heart Opening Exercises, n.d.).

To complete this exercise

1. Begin by standing upright.
2. Hold your arms to the front and with the palms of your hands facing each other.
3. Take a deep breath in and slowly pull your arms outward until you are able to clasp your hands behind your back.
4. Inhale several deep breaths until you feel your chest and shoulders expand.
5. Clench your shoulder blades together as you inhale.
6. Bring your arms to the front once more.
7. Repeat this exercise for a minimum of five sets.

If you find standing for this exercise difficult, complete it while sitting upright.

Practicing chest opener exercises is especially good for those of us who work at a desk and find ourselves hunched over a laptop or keyboard for hours. This exercise can strengthen our posture and back muscles. It will not only improve our upper body mobility but also contribute to an overall feeling of openness, such as physical, mental, and emotional.

Yoga Poses

Arm circles

Cat cow

Standing backbend

Standing forward fold

Standing sidebend

Chest opener

Neck Stretches

If you find that you are storing stress and anxiety in your neck, doing this stretch can help unwind tightness in these areas.

Begin by rotating your neck using the following instructions:

- Shift your head until you are focusing on the front.
- Tilt your head downward so that your chin rests against your chest.
- Hold this position for 10 counts. Take note of the stretching happening at the back of your neck.
- Lift your head and gently lay it to the left so that your ear is just above your shoulder.
- Hold this position for 10 counts and take note of the stretching of the right side of your neck.
- Shift your head to the back.
- Hold for 10 counts.
- Move your head to your right until it rests above your shoulder.
- Hold for 10 counts and note your neck stretching on the left side.
- Repeat this exercise five times.

Neck and Shoulder Stretch

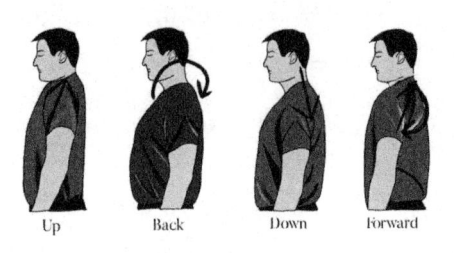

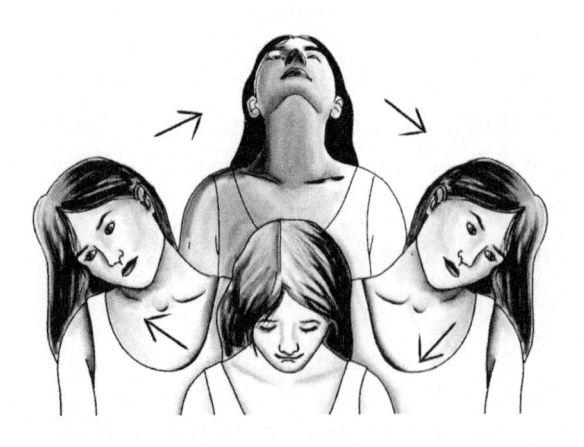

Up Back Down Forward

Shoulder Rolls

This exercise helps relieve pain, tension, and stress in the neck and shoulders. By bunching up and then slowly rolling your shoulders, you incorporate progressive muscle relaxation (PMR) techniques to release stiffness in these areas.

To complete shoulder rolls

1. Stand up straight or sit upright.
2. Lift your shoulder up to your jaw (or as far as you can reach)
3. Roll your shoulders to the back and bring them down.
4. Repeat this motion 10 times.

Safety Plan

Dear Reader,

It's common for people with depression to experience thoughts of suicide or self-harm. Active harmful thoughts may be expressed through statements such as "I wish I could take all my meds, go to sleep, and not wake up." Passive harmful thoughts may be expressed through these statements: *I wish I hadn't been born* or *My family would have been better off if I hadn't been here.*

When active harmful thoughts are rife, it's crucial to have a safety plan in place. A safety plan is a way to dial down feelings of acute distress and turn up feelings of hope. It ensures you're prepared with the tools and skills to see yourself safely through times of crisis.

Use the steps below to help develop your safety plan.

Step 1: Identify warning signs and trigger situations.

- Recognizing people, situations, thoughts, behaviors, or moods in advance enables you to avoid them or be better prepared for their unexpected arrival.

Step 2: Define healthy coping skills.

- Activate your parasympathetic nervous system (PNS) and decrease symptoms of arousal by cooling the temperature of your face. This can be done by placing a cool cloth on your face, using ice blocks, or having a refreshing cold shower.
- Begin paced (diaphragmatic) breathing to stimulate your PNS and reduce arousal.
- Incorporate progressive muscle relaxation (PMR) to create and release tension in your body and help it relax.
- Participate in intense physical activity. Engaging in any aerobic exercise or intense exercise for about 20 minutes increases your heart rate and releases endorphins, the feel-good hormone. Exercises that you can incorporate include running around the block, following a YouTube exercise video, or dancing to music.

Step 3: Making it through moments of crisis.

- When you feel a tidal wave of overwhelming emotions and harmful thoughts, distract and soothe yourself by removing yourself from the situation. Put on your comfort TV show, go outside in the sun, or talk to a friend.
- Create a hope box that contains items that bring you peace and joy and feed your dreams and desires for the future. This box can include pictures, letters, inspirational quotes, meaningful song lyrics, and a bucket list. Keep your hope box where it is visible and easily accessible.
- Eliminate dangerous objects such as scissors, blades, weapons, and medication from your environment. Place medication in an area not easily attainable in moments of crisis, or ask a family member to store it and dispense it when needed.

Step 4: Identify people to reach out to.

- Have a list of people and places that will shake up your routine, improve your socializing, make you feel good, distract you from your thoughts and problems, and relieve stress. These natural encounters will allow you to break away from negativity instead of mulling over it.
- In the event of a crisis, have a short list of trusted people whom you can call, who understand your situation, and whom you feel comfortable talking with about your suicidal thoughts. Close friends or

family members who can stay on the phone with you until the crisis passes.
- Call 911 or your local emergency number, or text TALK to 741741 to communicate with a trained crisis counselor.
- Make sure all numbers are readily available and accessible, and share your safety plan with your list of trusted people so that they know how best to help you.

Emotional pain can feel all-consuming and make it hard to see the light through the darkness, but these feelings will not last forever. Throughout this book, you have been learning skills that you can use to de-escalate this pain and re-engage with your life and the people who love you. Always remember: **You're not alone and you're worth it!**

Crisis and Suicide Awareness Protocol

Suppressed and unresolved trauma, perpetual triggers, and becoming trapped in a debilitating high-stress mental, emotional, and physical environment can feed active harmful thoughts to the point where suicide may seem like your only option of relief.

Suicide is one of the leading causes of death in the United States. At the end of 2023, statistics revealed that depression rates had increased from 19.6% in 2015 to 26% and that more than 50,000 Americans had died by suicide that year (Meet The Press, 2023). This all-time high number of suicides has revealed just how many people are not receiving the attentive care, comfort, and help needed to break free from trauma, addictions, depression, shame, and tormenting thoughts.

Suicide Prevention

Providing aid to someone at risk of self-harm or suicide goes a long way to helping them feel safe, wanted, or loved. If you know someone at immediate risk of performing these acts or hurting another person, here's what you can do (Leonard, 2020):

- Ask them whether they are considering suicide, such as "Are you considering suicide?"
- Listen to them without passing judgment.
- Dial 911 or your local emergency number.
- Alternatively, text TALK to 741741 to reach a trained crisis counselor.
- Stay with them until professional help arrives.
- Remove any visible potential harmful objects from them if it's safe to do so. This includes weapons, medications, or other potentially harmful objects.

If you or someone you know is experiencing suicidal thoughts or a crisis, dial 988 to reach the 24-hour National Suicide Prevention Lifeline. The 988 Suicide and Crisis Lifeline extends to the Department of Veterans Affairs (VA) and will provide assistance when you dial 988 and press 1 to reach the Veterans Crisis Line. During a crisis, people who are hard of hearing can use their preferred relay service or dial 711 then 988.

References

Andrade, S. (2021, July 1). *The importance of setting healthy boundaries*. Forbes. https://www.forbes.com/sites/forbescoachescouncil/2021/07/01/the-importance-of-setting-healthy-boundaries/?sh=5231b4ca56e4

Audice Wellness Services. (2023, August 20). *Pandulation: Practicing somatic relief at home for emotional well-being*. LinkedIn. https://www.linkedin.com/pulse/pandulation-practicing-somatic-release-home-emotional/?trk=article-ssr-frontend-pulse_more-articles_related-content-card

Baumgartner, B. (2019). *New mindful body awareness technique helps treat substance addiction, says UW study*. Northwest Dharma Association. https://northwestdharma.org/mindadd/

Basile, L. M. (2020, September 3). *How trauma impacts your physical health*. Health Central. https://www.healthcentral.com/chronic-health/how-trauma-impacts-your-health

Bass, E. (n.d.). *Emotional freedom quotes*. Goodreads. https://www.goodreads.com/quotes/tag/emotional-freedom

Barkley, S. (2023, May 3). *17 Inspiring quotes about setting healthy boundaries*. PsychCentral. https://psychcentral.com/health/quotes-healthy-boundaries

Bedosky, L. (2022, November 9). *What is EFT tapping? A detailed scientific guide on emotional freedom technique*. Everyday Health. https://www.everydayhealth.com/wellness/eft-tapping/guide/

Brooks, D. (n.d.). *8 Somatic Breathing Exercises to do today*. Original Body Wisdom. https://originalbodywisdom.com/8-somatic-breathing-exercises-to-do-today/

Cenizal, C. (2022, November 11). *Riding out emotional waves*. CJ Cenizal. https://www.cenizal.com/riding-out-emotional-waves/

Chamberlain, J. (2023, August 17). *Somatic therapy: How it works and what to expect*. Choosing Therapy. https://www.choosingtherapy.com/somatic-therapy/

Chalica, E. (2023). *11 Somatic grounding exercises for when you need to manage your triggers*. BetterMe. https://betterme.world/articles/somatic-grounding-exercises/

Chateau Health & Wellness. (2023, September 21). *Understanding trauma-informed care: A holistic approach to healing for first responders*. Chateau Health & Wellness. https://www.chateaurecovery.com/understanding-trauma-informed-care-a-holistic-approach-to-healing-for-first-responders

Cleveland Clinic. (2023, September 6). *Exposure therapy*. Cleveland Clinic. https://my.clevelandclinic.org/health/treatments/25067-exposure-therapy

Cohen, E. (2023, November 10). *How somatic breathwork can help you chill out*. Charlie Health. https://www.charliehealth.com/post/somatic-breathwork

Corcoran, C. (2024, February 5). *EMDR therapy for trauma, ptsd, anxiety, and panic*. HelpGuide.org. https://www.helpguide.org/articles/therapy-medication/emdr-therapy.htm

Darvasula, R. (2022, July 12). *9 Signs of poor boundaries (and what to do instead)*. MedCircle. https://medcircle.com/articles/signs-of-poor-boundaries/

David, M. (2015, February 18). *Resourcing in trauma therapy: An antidote to traumatic activation*. The Institute for the Psychology of Eating. https://psychologyofeating.com/resourcing-antidote-traumatic-activation/

Egel, K. (2021, March 2). *6 Signs of a body, mind & spirit disconnect*. Kim Egel. https://www.kimegel.com/blog/2021/2/12/6-signs-of-body-mind-amp-spirit-disconnect

Erieau, C. (2019, February 20). *The 50 best resilience quotes*. Driven. https://home.hellodriven.com/articles/the-50-best-resilience-quotes/

Fountaine, S. (2020, January 21). *100 Grounding quotes*. Feasting at Home. https://www.feastingathome.com/100-inspirational-quotes/

Gordon, S. (2023, October 5). *What is grounding?* Health. https://www.health.com/grounding-7968373#:

Hadley, H. (2023, July 19). *The benefits of somatic breathing*. Total Somatics. https://totalsomatics.com/the-benefits-of-somatic-breathing/

Hamilton, L. K. (n.d.). Trauma quotes. Goodreads. https://www.goodreads.com/quotes/tag/trauma

Hanson, H. (2014, July 16). *13 Benefits of pendulation for healing from trauma (pendulation article 4)*. New-Synapse. https://www.new-synapse.com/aps/wordpress/?p=542

Hanson, H. (2016, May 28). *On the importance of titration for trauma healing (10 benefits)*. New-Synapse. https://www.new-synapse.com/aps/wordpress/?p=1842

Heart opening exercises. (n.d.). Blackroll. https://blackroll.com/routine/heart-opening-exercises

Hillesum, E. (2023, July 29). *Breathe quotes: 10 Inspirational sayings to help you find inner peace*. Blinkist Magazine. https://www.blinkist.com/magazine/posts/breathe-quotes-10-inspirational-sayings-help-find-inner-peace?utm_source=cpp

Hills, A. (2023, April 19). *Breathwork for trauma and ptsd: A healing approach*. Breathless. https://breathlessexpeditions.com/breathwork-for-trauma-and-ptsd/

Hodgson, T. (2022, December 9). *Standing forward bend*. Yoga Journal. https://www.yogajournal.com/poses/standing-forward-bend-2/

Holland, T. M. (2018, January 24). *What is holistic health care, anyway?* Dignity Health. https://www.dignityhealth.org/articles/what-is-holistic-health-care-anyway

Integrative Life Center. (2022, May 5). *Benefits of somatic therapy*. Integrative Life Center. https://integrativelifecenter.com/therapy-services/benefits-of-somatic-therapy/

Jacobs, S. (2023, February 1). *Addressing body image concerns using mirror exposure*. Behavioral Psych Studio. https://behavioralpsychstudio.com/addressing-body-image-concerns-using-mirror-exposure/

Jacobson, S. (2023, March 4). *Buried treasure: Finding your inner resources*. Harley Therapy. https://www.harleytherapy.co.uk/counselling/find-your-inner-resources.htm

Khoddam, R. (2021, March 3). *How trauma affects the body*. Psychology Today. https://www.psychologytoday.com/intl/blog/the-addiction-connection/202103/how-trauma-affects-the-body

Khoddam, R. (2023, January 11). *Grounding techniques for trauma and anxiety*. Psychology Today. https://www.psychologytoday.com/intl/blog/the-addiction-connection/202301/grounding-techniques-for-trauma-and-anxiety

Kinsmen, J. (2020, March 11). *Feelings are much like waves, we can't stop them from coming, but we can choose which one to surf'—Jonatan Mårtensson*. LinkedIn. https://www.linkedin.com/pulse/feelings-much-like-waves-we-cant-stop-them-from-coming-juliet-kinsman/

Kirstein, M. (2023, November 2). *7 Best somatic breathwork exercises for stress-relief*. Mona Kirstein. https://www.monakirstein.com/somatic-breathwork/

Kryger, Kelsey. "75 Healing Quotes To Help You Through Loss, Trauma and

Grief." Parade.com. Last modified April 12, 2023. https://parade.com/living/healing-quotes.

Lebow, H. I. (2023, January 21). *How does your body remember trauma?* PsychCentral. https://psychcentral.com/health/how-your-body-remembers-trauma#trauma-and-the-body

Lee, K. (2018, September 11). *Why is it so hard to set boundaries?* Psychology Today. https://www.psychologytoday.com/us/blog/rethink-your-way-the-good-life/201809/why-is-it-so-hard-set-boundaries

Levine, P. (2010). *In an unspoken voice; how the body releases trauma and restores goodness.* North Atlantic Books.

Leonard, J. (2020, June 3). *What is trauma? What to know.* Medical News Today. https://www.medicalnewstoday.com/articles/trauma#definition

Lewis, T. (n.d.). *Top 13 somatic therapy quotes.* Quote Stats. https://quotestats.com/topic/somatic-therapy-quotes/

Lindberg, S. (2023, February 14). *What is talk therapy and can it help?* Healthline. https://www.healthline.com/health/mental-health/talk-therapy#types

Lockett, E. (2023, March 27). *Grounding: Exploring earthing science and the benefits behind it.* Healthline. https://www.healthline.com/health/grounding

Mazzei, R. (2021, January 7). *What is resourcing in emdr therapy?* Evolutions Behavioral Health Services. https://www.evolutionsbh.com/articles/what-is-resourcing-in-emdr-therapy/

Meet The Press. (2023, December 31). More than 50,000 died by suicide in 2023—more than any year of record. NBC News. https://www.nbcnews.com/meet-the-press/video/more-than-50-000-americans-died-by-suicide-in-2023-more-than-any-year-on-record-201161285832

McDonald, J. M. (2024, March 14). 58 healing quotes for inspiration and encouragement. Southern Living. https://www.southernliving.com/culture/healing-quotes

Moore, M. (2022, August 29). *How to mend porous boundaries, today.* Psych Central. https://psychcentral.com/relationships/signs-your-boundaries-are-too-loose-or-too-rigid#a-closer-look

Morgan, K. (2021, September 7). *How to overcome trauma with body awareness and embodiment.* Red Beard. https://www.redbeardsomatictherapy.com/post/hot-to-overcome-trauma-with-body-awareness-and-embodiment

Pagán, C. N. (2018, November 29). *When you're emotionally affected by trauma*. WebMD. https://www.webmd.com/mental-health/features/emotional-trauma-aftermath

Pattemore, C. (2021, June 3). *10 ways to build and preserve better boundaries*. Psych Central. https://psychcentral.com/lib/10-way-to-build-and-preserve-better-boundaries

Perry, M. (2023, March 21). *How to start journaling for mental health: 7 tips and techniques*. BetterUp. https://www.betterup.com/blog/how-to-start-journaling#how-to-start-journaling-(and-make-it-a-habit)

Pizer, A. (2018, April 27). *How to do mountain pose (tadasana)*. Liforme. https://liforme.com/blogs/blog/how-to-do-mountain-pose-tadasana

Porrey, M. (2024, Feb 1). *Types and uses of somatic trauma therapy*. VeryWell Mind. https://www.verywellhealth.com/somatic-trauma-therapy-5218970

Porter, S. (2023, May 11). *Trauma triggers: How to identify & deal with them*. Choosing Therapy. https://www.choosingtherapy.com/trauma-triggers/

Princing, M. (2021, September 1). *This is why deep breathing makes you feel so chill*. Right As Rain. https://rightasrain.uwmedicine.org/mind/stress/why-deep-breathing-makes-you-feel-so-chill

Raypole, C. (2024, January, 29). *30 Grounding techniques to quiet distressing thoughts*. Healthline. https://www.healthline.com/health/grounding-techniques

Redman, C. (2021, May 6). *Self-resourcing: You've got this*. Colorado Center for Couple and Families. https://coloradocouples.com/self-resourcing-youve-got-this/

Resnick, A. (2023, November 7). *What is somatic therapy?* VeryWell Mind. https://www.verywellmind.com/what-is-somatic-therapy-5190064

Robboy, A. (n.d.). *Identifying your boundaries*. The Center for Growth. https://www.thecenterforgrowth.com/tips/identifying-your-boundaries

Sabater, V. (2023, May 8). *The pendulation technique for managing anguish*. Exploring Your Mind. https://exploringyourmind.com/pendulation-technique-for-managing-anguish/

Salamon, M. (2023, July 7). *What is somatic therapy?* Harvard Health Publishing. https://www.health.harvard.edu/blog/what-is-somatic-therapy-202307072951

Schmelzer, G. (2015, January 21). *Box it up or let it flow: Titrating emotion*. Gretchen Schmelzer. https://gretchenschmelzer.com/blog-1/2015/1/21/box-it-up-or-let-it-flow-titrating-emotion#:

Scott. E. (2024, February 12). *What is body scan meditation?* VeryWell Mind. https://www.verywellmind.com/body-scan-meditation-why-and-how-3144782

Sharpe, R. (2021, February 27). *100+ PTSD quotes to help survivors cope with trauma.* Declutter The Mind. https://declutterthemind.com/blog/ptsd-quotes/

Silva, L. (2024, January 25). *What is somatic therapy? Benefits, types and more.* Forbes Health. https://www.forbes.com/health/mind/somatic-therapy/

Smith Haghighi, A. (2021, March 9). *What to know about creative therapy.* Medical News Today. https://www.medicalnewstoday.com/articles/creative-therapy

Smith-Hayduk, K. (2022, December 7). *Researchers reveal how trauma changes the brain.* Rochester Medical Center. https://www.urmc.rochester.edu/news/publications/neuroscience/researchers-reveal-how-trauma-changes-the-brain

Stöppler, M. C. (2022, January 2022). *Progressive muscle relaxation for stress and insomnia.* WebMD. https://www.webmd.com/sleep-disorders/muscle-relaxation-for-stress-insomnia

Tartakovsky, M. (2014, February 26). *How to figure out your boundaries.* Psych Central. https://psychcentral.com/health/how-to-make-days-go-by-faster#tips

Tolle, E. (n.d.). *Body awareness quotes.* Goodreads. https://www.goodreads.com/quotes/tag/body-awareness

Tomasello, C. (2021, August, 27). *3 Ways that emotions are like a wave.* Beachside Counseling. https://www.beachsidecounseling.com/post/3-ways-that-emotions-are-like-a-wave

Tucker, L. (2023, October 11). *Somatic breathwork: The benefits of slow breathing.* Neurology Advisor. https://www.neurologyadvisor.com/topics/general-neurology/the-benefits-of-slow-breathing/

Van Horn, H. (2023, July 12). *How journaling about trauma can help.* Day One. https://dayoneapp.com/blog/journaling-about-trauma/#:

Van Derbur, M. (n.d.). *Somatic therapy quotes.* Goodreads. https://www.goodreads.com/quotes/tag/somatic-therapy

What is the importance of holistic healing therapy? (2021, July 5). Fazlani Nature's Nest. https://fazlaninaturesnest.com/what-is-the-importance-of-holistic-healing-therapy/#:

Youst, J. (2016). *9 Somatic breath techniques.* The Power of Breath Institute. https://empoweryourmindset.org/wp-content/uploads/2020/06/9-SOMATIC-BREATH-TECHNIQUES.pdf

Zapata, A. (2021, August 31). *6 Ways to connect to your inner resources.* Healing House. https://www.dallashealinghouse.com/blog/2021/8/4/5-ways-to-connect-to-your-inner-resources

Zuda Yoga. (2023, February 28). *Standing cat cow and four other amazing poses to get you through your day.* Zuda Yoga. https://zudayoga.com/standing-cat-cow-4-other-poses-to-get-through-your-day